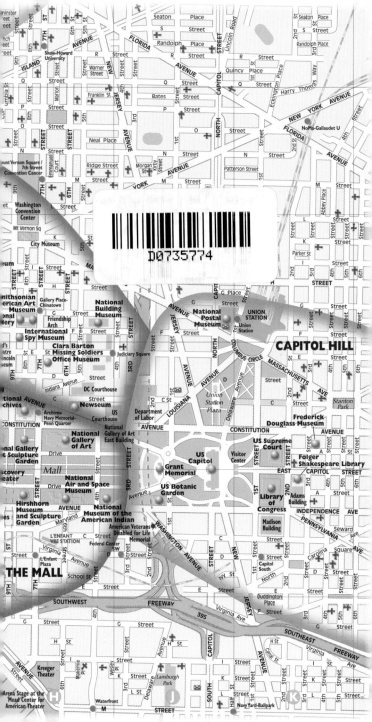

How to Use This Book

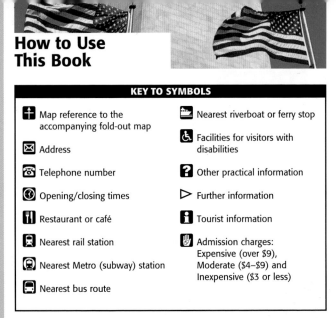

KEY TO SYMBOLS	
✚ Map reference to the accompanying fold-out map	🚢 Nearest riverboat or ferry stop
✉ Address	♿ Facilities for visitors with disabilities
☎ Telephone number	❓ Other practical information
⏰ Opening/closing times	▷ Further information
🍽 Restaurant or café	ℹ Tourist information
🚆 Nearest rail station	🖐 Admission charges: Expensive (over $9), Moderate ($4–$9) and Inexpensive ($3 or less)
Ⓜ Nearest Metro (subway) station	
🚌 Nearest bus route	

This guide is divided into four sections

• **Essential Washington:** An introduction to the city and tips on making the most of your stay.
• **Washington by Area:** We've broken the city into six areas, and recommended the best sights, shops, entertainment venues, nightlife and places to eat in each one. Suggested walks help you to explore on foot. Farther Afield takes you out of the city.
• **Where to Stay:** The best hotels, whether you're looking for luxury, budget or something in between.
• **Need to Know:** The info you need to make your trip run smoothly, including getting about by public transportation, weather tips, emergency phone numbers and useful websites.

Navigation In the Washington by Area chapter, we've given each area its own color, which is also used on the locator maps throughout the book and the map on the inside front cover.

Maps The fold-out map with this book is a comprehensive street plan of Washington. The grid on this fold-out map is the same as the grid on the locator maps within the book. We've given grid references within the book for each sight and listing.

Contents

CONTENTS

Introducing Washington

An equal mix of Southern gentility and Northern sophistication, America's capital is a microcosm of the United States, the melting pot's melting pot. Washington DC is both quintessentially American and unique as an American city.

Washington is a city that was founded on politics because it was a compromise from the start. The site, close to George Washington's home at Mount Vernon, was chosen after a deal was brokered for the South to pay the North's revolutionary war debts in exchange for having a southern capital. Virginia and Maryland donated land, and architect Pierre Charles L'Enfant (1754–1825) designed a city with a focal triangle formed by the Capitol, the president's house and a statue where the Washington Monument now sits.

L'Enfant also included plans for the Mall and diagonal boulevards crossing the grid of streets. L'Enfant's magnificent vision can be appreciated now, but for a long time the city was sparsely populated with unpaved avenues. Cattle grazed on the Mall and America's famous early leaders lived and worked in dank, dilapidated buildings.

This city is rich in things to see. Capitol Hill and the Mall, replete with free museums, galleries and monuments, exhibit the range of America's wealth and artistry. The revitalized U Street and Columbia Heights reveal its cultural dynamism. Embassies have brought foreign delegations and friends, imbuing this relatively small city with pockets of cuisine and culture unavailable elsewhere in the US. And the arts scene, in part fueled by the droves of young professionals that move to the capital clamoring for powerful positions, is sophisticated.

But although different types of businesses are moving to the city and helping to invigorate it, its core business remains government.

FACTS AND FIGURES

● The 230ft (70m) escalator at the Wheaton Metro station, in Montgomery County, is the longest in the western hemisphere.

● The Pentagon, at 6.6 million ft (613,000sq m), is the world's third-largest building by floor area and has nearly 17.5 miles (28.2km) of corridors and 131 stairways.

TAXATION, REPRESENTATION?

Washington DC license plates read "Taxation without Representation," a familiar refrain from the Revolutionary War. In this case the term alludes to the fact that the District lacks a voting representative in Congress. To add insult to injury, the Constitution also specifically gives Congress control over Washington's entire budget.

DC ON FIRE

On August 24, 1814, as part of the ongoing War of 1812, British soldiers entered Washington and began torching the town. They destroyed many buildings, including the Capitol and the White House, but not before dining on a feast First Lady Dolley Madison had hubristically prepared before being forced to leave. Both buildings still retain scars from the incident.

SECOND SUBWAY

Members of Congress in a rush to vote need not break a sweat. In 1909, underground subway cars were installed to traverse the little more than 500ft (150m) between the Russell Senate Office Building and the Capitol. As subsequent office buildings were added, so were more train lines. These cars, most still open-top, continue to operate today.

A Short Stay in Washington

DAY 1

Morning Start your day at **Union Station** (▷ 66) and grab some coffee in the food court or a more substantial breakfast at the café in the main hall. Follow the flood of "Hill staffers" (▷ 123) as they head to work just before 9am. Most of them will stop at the Senate Office Buildings. You should, too, if you have arranged a tour in advance. Otherwise head to the Capitol Visitor Center at the **Capitol** (▷ 60) and take a tour.

Lunch Head west out of the Capitol and onto the Mall. Either enjoy a meal of Native American delicacies at the **National Museum of the American Indian** (▷ 44) or lunch at the Cascade Café, with a view of the waterfall, at the **National Gallery of Art** (▷ 41).

Afternoon Stay on after lunch and take in an exhibition at either museum, neither of which will disappoint.

Mid-afternoon Walk west along the Mall past the Smithsonian museums to the **Washington Monument** (▷ 46). Head up to the top (it's best to reserve tickets in advance) to catch a spectacular view of the city. On returning to earth walk due north to **The White House** (▷ 25).

Dinner Walk up to Farragut North Metro station and take the train downtown to the Gallery Place–Chinatown Metro station. Head west on G Street for Mediterranean tapas at the light, airy and lively **Zaytinya** (▷ 32).

Evening After dinner, stop for a drink at the patio at **Poste** (▷ 30) before taking in a show at the **Shakespeare Theatre** (▷ 30) or **Woolly Mammoth** (▷ 30), depending on whether you like the Bard or avant garde.

DAY 2

Morning Start off the day at the **National Zoological Park** (▷ 84). Be sure to say hello to the pandas, the orangutans on the "O line" and the Komodo dragon, the first to be born outside of Indonesia.

Mid-morning Walk south on Connecticut Avenue and hop on the Metro to **Dupont Circle** (▷ 88). Or, if you stayed only a short time at the zoo, walk across the Calvert Street Bridge instead and take an immediate right down 18th Street through Adams Morgan.

Lunch If it's warm, try one of the outdoor cafés near Dupont Circle Metro's north entrance at Q Street or on 17th Street, or take a picnic to the Circle. There are also many good indoor options on Connecticut Avenue north and south of the Circle, and on P Street west of the Circle.

Afternoon Take the Metro to the Smithsonian station. Walk toward the **Washington Monument** (▷ 46) to 15th Street SW and take a left, heading toward the Tidal Basin, where you will find the **Martin Luther King, Jr., Roosevelt** and **Jefferson memorials** (▷ 36, 38).

Mid-afternoon Walk from the FDR Memorial north to the Reflecting Pool and the **Lincoln Memorial** (▷ 37), where Martin Luther King, Jr. delivered his "I Have a Dream" speech in 1963.

Dinner Enjoy the carefully crafted food at the restaurants in the **Mandarin Oriental hotel** (▷ 112): **Muze** (▷ 52) for great views or the Empress Lounge if you're looking for something more casual.

Evening Catch a taxi to the **John F. Kennedy Center** (▷ 74), where, depending on the night, you can choose between ballet, opera, the symphony orchestra and world-class theater.

►►►

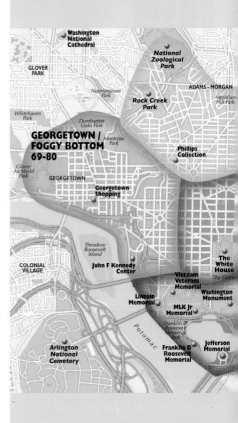

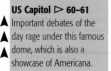

These pages are a quick guide to the Top 25, which are described in more detail later. Here they are listed alphabetically, and the tinted background shows which area they are in.

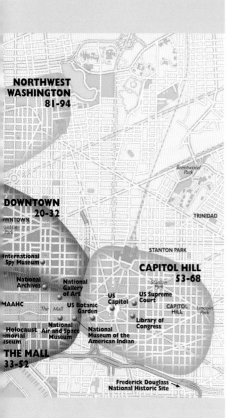

NORTHWEST WASHINGTON 81–94

DOWNTOWN 20–32

WNTOWN ankin Park

International Spy Museum

National Archives

National Gallery of Art

MAAHC

US Botanic Garden

The Mall

Holocaust emorial useum

National Air and Space Museum

National Museum of the American Indian

THE MALL 33–52

Brentwood Park

TRINIDAD

STANTON PARK

CAPITOL HILL 53–68

Stanton Park

US Capitol

US Supreme Court

CAPITOL HILL

Lincoln Park

Library of Congress

Frederick Douglass National Historic Site

Shopping

For those who see DC as a serious place, the abundance of shopping options, from high-end showrooms to chic boutiques, might come as a surprise.

Shopping Areas

Those with style and the money to prove it will find shops like Caroline Herrera, Paul Stuart and Hermes in Downtown's CityCenterDC complex, with Chanel, Tiffany and Co. and Neiman-Marcus located in Friendship Heights and Chevy Chase. Vintage hunters can rummage for deals along the Adams Morgan strip, on U Street or in Eastern Market on Capitol Hill. Mainstreamers will find solace in their favorite stores in Downtown, Georgetown and Pentagon City. Antiques and art hounds should head to Georgetown or Dupont Circle. Fashionable but hard-to-find styles for body and home can be found on Book Hill in Georgetown, along 14th Street and on U Street.

Bookworms

This city has not shortchanged its policy experts, think tanks and foundations with a lack of reading material. You'll find two major chains—Barnes and Noble and Books-a-Million—are well-represented, but bookworms will also find some unbeatable independents, such as Kramerbooks and Politics & Prose, that often include comfortable cafés and reading areas among their eclectic collections. Bridge Street Books in Georgetown and Upshur Books in Petworth are smaller but well-stocked options.

Broaden the Mind

In fact, DC is generally the place to go if you're looking for something to broaden your mind.

AFRICAN AND ASIAN INFLUENCES

Two Smithsonian museums, the National Museum of African Art (africa.si.edu) and Arthur M. Sackler Gallery (asia.si.edu), carry a variety of decorative arts, jewelry, handicrafts and clothing in their gift shops.

Georgetown (top and middle) and the window display of the French Market (bottom)

Aside from being a visual feast for students of all ages, the city's many museums and galleries contain gift shops and bookstores that extend the experience and learning process. The National Museum of the American Indian stocks an expansive collection of Native American crafts, games and books. The National Building Museum carries a huge library of books on DC and the building arts. Many art museums around town, including the National Gallery of Art and the Hirshhorn, sell items ranging from exhibit catalogs to artisanal jewelry and high-quality prints. The National Museum of Natural History stocks everything from beautiful home-ware to science kits. And don't forget that the National Air and Space Museum sells items for budding astronauts—glow-in-the-dark stars and freeze-dried astronaut food.

Memorabilia
Likewise, nearly every government building and monument—including the White House, the Capitol, the Library of Congress and the Lincoln Memorial—sells American memorabilia.

Local Delights
A growing Made In DC movement promotes homegrown businesses and locally produced products. The website of the non-profit Think Local First is an excellent resource for finding a variety of district-based shops, cafés, artisanal foods and services.

Georgetown (top); Chanel store (top middle); fresh crabs (middle); stylish shoes (bottom)

POLITICAL EPHEMERA

Election year or not, DC is a ready source of campaign ephemera—buttons, bumper stickers, matchbooks with party logos and the like. At bookstores, museum gift shops and street vendors, reproductions and original memorabilia abound. Looking for pewter flatware and candlesticks used by 18th-century administrations? A tacky T-shirt commenting on the latest Washington scandal? Who can resist the salt and pepper shakers shaped like the Washington Monument or campaign buttons designed for FDR? For this kind of Americana, there's no place like DC.

Shopping by Theme

Whether you're looking for a department store, a quirky boutique or something in between, you'll find it all in Washington. On this page shops are listed by theme. For a more detailed write-up, see the individual listings in Washington by Area.

Art and Antiques
Claude Taylor Photography (▷ 90)
Hemphill Fine Arts (▷ 90)
Jean Pierre Antiques (▷ 77)
National Gallery of Art (▷ 52)
The Old Print Gallery (▷ 77)
Torpedo Factory Art Center (▷ 104)

Beauty and Skincare
Blue Mercury (▷ 90)
Grooming Lounge (▷ 29)
Kiehl's (▷ 78)

Books
Bridge Street Books (▷ 77)
Capitol Hill Books (▷ 66)
Kramerbooks (▷ 91)
Reiter's Books (▷ 29)
Second Story Books (▷ 91)

Craft and Stationery
Beadazzled (▷ 90)
Fahrney's Pens (▷ 29)
Groovy dc Cards & Gifts (▷ 66)
Just Paper and Tea (▷ 78)
Paper Source (▷ 78)

Food and Wine
A. Litteri (▷ 66)
Calvert Woodley Liquors (▷ 90)
Dean and Deluca (▷ 77)
Eastern Market (▷ 64, 66)
Glen's Garden Market (▷ 90)

For Kids
Fairy Godmother (▷ 66)
National Air and Space Museum (▷ 52)
National Museum of the American Indian (▷ 52)
National Museum of Natural History (▷ 52)

Home Furnishings
A Mano (▷ 77)
Anthropologie (▷ 77)
Design Within Reach (▷ 77)
Good Wood (▷ 90)
Home Rule (▷ 90)
Miss Pixie's (▷ 91)
Tabletop (▷ 91)
Woven History and Silk Road (▷ 66)

Malls
CityCenterDC (▷ 29)
Fashion Centre (▷ 104)
Friendship Heights (▷ 104)
Gallery Place (▷ 29)
Potomac Mills Mall (▷ 104)

Tanger Outlets (▷ 104)
Tysons Corner (▷ 104)
Union Station (▷ 66)

Menswear
Alden (▷ 29)
J. Press (▷ 29)

Music
Crooked Beat Records (▷ 90)
House of Musical Traditions (▷ 104)
Smash Records (▷ 91)

Womenswear
2nd Time Around (▷ 77)
Anthropologie (▷ 77)
Betsy Fisher (▷ 90)
Coup de Foudre (▷ 29)
Forecast (▷ 66)
Hu's Shoes (▷ 77)
Intermix (▷ 77)
Meeps (▷ 91)
Nordstrom Rack (▷ 29)
Proper Topper (▷ 29, 91)
Rizik's (▷ 91)
Secondi (▷ 91)

The mix of bustling restaurants, bars serving craft beer and handcrafted cocktails, arts venues and year-round sports events makes Washington a vibrant place at night. Hot spots around town are busy early and stay open late even on some weeknights, especially in the warmer months when people seek outdoor and rooftop seating.

Going Out

Young professionals tend to head to areas like H Street and 14th Street, the hot spots of the moment; Dupont Circle; Adams Morgan, which can get overcrowded with the 20-something crowd; Capitol Hill, which provides quick access after work; and the area around the Clarendon Metro stop in Arlington, where many Hill staffers (▷ 123) live. The myriad bars, cafés, live music venues, theaters and cinemas means there is something for everyone not only in downtown DC, but also in its near by neighborhoods and suburbs.

Monuments in the Moonlight

Perhaps the most inspiring, memorable evening experiences happen outdoors. The monuments and memorials, glorious in the sunlight, are entrancing in the moonlight. The Capitol looms on its hill over the Mall. The Lincoln Memorial stands guard at one end of Memorial Bridge, as does the Jefferson Memorial at the Tidal Basin. And the stark white Washington Monument is visible from most points in town. Tours by bus, Segway, bike, boat and foot bring these iconic sights to life. Visit the tourist information office for more on guided tours.

SCREEN ON THE GREEN

On Monday nights throughout July and August the Mall in Downtown is turned into a free open-air cinema screening films from Hollywood classics to more recent favorites. Washingtonians arrive as early as 5pm to save a spot and picnic on the lawn stretching between 4th and 7th streets (hbo.com/screenonthegreen).

Some of the many ways to spend an evening in Washington (above)

Eating Out

The Washington dining scene has come into its own in recent years as more and more residents have moved into the city and neighborhoods once deemed undesirable have become crowded with new cafés and restaurants. Fine dining, farm-to-table fare, small plates, upmarket hamburgers, tasting menus—it's all here.

Top Chefs

Benefiting from lush swaths of nearby farmland and the seafood-rich Chesapeake Bay, the undeniable talent of chefs like José Andrés (at Zaytinya, Jaleo and Oyamel), Cathal Armstrong (at Restaurant Eve) and Michel Richard (at Central) are taking cuisine to new levels. Their restaurants and others are no longer simply "good for DC". They're objectively a treat. Chefs like Spike Mendelson (Good Stuff Eatery) and Mike Isabella (Graffiato) have gained fame on TV, as has Carla Hall, who trained as a chef in DC. Reservations are usually recommended at most establishments, unless a "no reservations" policy is followed, which is an increasingly popular trend.

International Cuisine

The city's diverse population has spawned an equally diverse restaurant scene. Home to many Ethiopians, DC dishes out its fair share of this East African cuisine, especially in Adams Morgan and Shaw. Likewise, a sizeable El Salvadorian crowd has set up restaurants and *pupuserias* in Mount Pleasant and Columbia Heights. In addition, West African, Thai, Chinese, Greek, Lebanese and Indian cuisines, among countless others, put up a good fight for their fair share of restaurant space.

RESTAURANT WEEK

For a week each January and August, a host of DC's restaurants, including some of its finest, offer three course, fixed-price lunch and dinner menus for less than $50. Make reservations well in advance (ramw.org).

Fruit salad (top); fusion food and fine cuisine (middle); alfresco dining (bottom)

Where to Eat by Cuisine

There are plenty of places to eat to suit all tastes and budgets in Washington. On this page they are listed by cuisine. For a more detailed description of each venue, see Washington by Area.

American
Central (▷ 31)
CF Folks (▷ 93)
Clyde's (▷ 31)
Corduroy (▷ 31)
Equinox (▷ 31)
Founding Farmers (▷ 31)
Good Stuff Eatery (▷ 68)
Grapeseed (▷ 106)
Inn at Little Washington (▷ 106)
Komi (▷ 94)
NOPA Kitchen and Bar (▷ 32)
Nora (▷ 94)
Range (▷ 106)
Restaurant Eve (▷ 106)
Rose's Luxury (▷ 68)
Ted's Bulletin (▷ 68)

Asian
Miss Saigon (▷ 80)
Muze (▷ 52)
Pho 75 (▷ 106)
Sushi Taro (▷ 94)
Teaism (▷ 94)
Thai Chef (▷ 94)

Burgers
Five Guys (▷ 31)
Ray's Hell Burger (▷ 106)
Satellite (▷ 94)

Casual
Amsterdam Falafelshop (▷ 93)
Ben's Chili Bowl (▷ 93)
Busboys and Poets (▷ 93)

European
Belga Café (▷ 68)
Leopold's Kafe and Konditorei (▷ 80)

French
Bistro Français (▷ 80)
Chez Billy Sud (▷ 80)
Le Diplomate (▷ 93)
Montmartre (▷ 68)

Indian
Indique (▷ 94)
Masala Art (▷ 52)
Rasika (▷ 32)

Italian
Centrolina (▷ 31)
Graffiato (▷ 32)

Latin
Banana Café and Piano Bar (▷ 68)

Mediterranean
Fiola Mare (▷ 80)
Jaleo (▷ 32)
Kellari Taverna (▷ 32)
Lebanese Taverna (▷ 94)
Mezè (▷ 94)
Zaytinya (▷ 32)

Mexican
Oyamel (▷ 32)

Picnics, Soups & Sandwiches
Breadline (▷ 31)
Firehook (▷ 68)
Pavilion Café (▷ 52)

Pizza
Matchbox (▷ 32)
Pizzeria Paradiso (▷ 80)

Pub Food
Brixton (▷ 93)

Seafood
1789 (▷ 80)
Granville Moore's (▷ 106)
Hank's Oyster Bar (▷ 94)
Market Lunch (▷ 68)

Steak
Bourbon Steak (▷ 80)
The Prime Rib (▷ 32)
Ray's the Steaks (▷ 106)

West African
Bukom Café (▷ 93)

Top Tips For...

These great suggestions will help you tailor your ideal visit to Washington, no matter how you choose to spend your time. Each sight or listing has a fuller write-up elsewhere in the book.

A BIRD'S-EYE VIEW

Look over Downtown, the Capitol (▷ 60) and the Mall from the Capitol Terrace observation deck of the Newseum (▷ 27).
Sip cocktails at the POV roof terrace of the W Hotel (▷ 30) with a magnificent view of the Washington Monument.
Enjoy the 360-degree panorama over the Potomac and Foggy Bottom from the John F. Kennedy Center's terraces (▷ 74).

TRAIPSING AROUND TOWN IN FANCY SHOES

Peruse Hu's Shoes (▷ 77), an unparalleled selection of high-end women's footwear.
Or decide not to pay a fortune for a pair of shoes and instead go to Nordstrom Rack (▷ 29) for some real bargains.

DINING OUT OF THE BOX

Sample Austrian cuisine and mouth-watering pastries at Leopold's Kafe and Konditorei (▷ 80).
Enjoy the fresh flavors at Nora (▷ 94), America's first certified organic restaurant.

PEOPLE-WATCHING

Sit by the fire in the Ritz-Carlton (▷ 112) and spend time people-watching the ambassadors, politicos and sheiks.
Drink in the history in the ornate lobby of the Willard Intercontinental (▷ 112), a short walk from the White House.

The Capitol (above); Hu's Shoes (below); Willard Intercontinental Hotel (bottom)

Spa pampering (below); music at the Kennedy Center (middle)

BEING PAMPERED

Soak up the shaving lather in the plush Grooming Lounge (▷ 29).
Get the full treatment at the soothing spa in the Mandarin Oriental (▷ 112).
Enjoy the wellness-themed rooms, morning smoothies and yoga channel at Topaz Hotel (▷ 111), located in Dupont.

WATCHING WORLD-CLASS THEATER

Enjoy superbly acted and staged plays by Shakespeare and his peers at the Shakespeare Theatre (▷ 30).
Catch the world's best touring acts—from theater to music to dance—at the regal John F. Kennedy Center (▷ 74).
Go back in time and glimpse the avant garde at the home of the Woolly Mammoth Theatre Company (▷ 30).

KEEPING MONEY IN YOUR POCKET

Visit the city's free locations, from the National Zoological Park (▷ 84), through all the Smithsonian museums to the National Gallery of Art (▷ 41).
Explore the more than 1,700 acres (687ha) of Rock Creek Park's recreational space (▷ 86).

Rock Creek cyclists (above); fine wines on offer at Washington's bars (below)

A GREAT SELECTION AT THE BAR

Sip one of the bartenders' expert recommendations at Sonoma Wine Bar (▷ 67).
Wet your whistle with the world's best beers at Birreria Paradiso (▷ 78).
Try a pint of Belgium's finest at Belga Café (▷ 68).

KEEPING YOUR KIDS OCCUPIED

National Museum of Natural History (below)

Let them create their own structures at the National Building Museum's Building Zone (▷ 26).

Playfully interact with exhibits in Wonderplace at the National Museum of American History (▷ 50).

Help feed a tarantula at the National Museum of Natural History's Insect Zoo (▷ 50).

Let the Smithsonian Discovery Theater (▷ 49) dazzle with puppet shows, music and storytelling.

EATING WHERE LOCALS EAT

Take comfort in breakfast served all day at Ted's Bulletin (▷ 68).

Breathe in the smell of freshly baked bread and cakes at Firehook (▷ 68).

GETTING OUTDOORS

Follow the tree-lined towpath along the Chesapeake & Ohio (C&O) Canal (▷ 75), through the forest from Georgetown to Maryland.

Wander among trees from almost every state at the National Arboretum (▷ 102).

Enjoy the verdant Bishop's Garden (▷ 88) in the shadow of the National Cathedral (▷ 87).

Towpath of the Chesapeake & Ohio Canal (above middle); not just trees at the National Arboretum (above)

SHOPPING WITH THE CHIC SET

Smell the flowers, sample the cheese and then sip a cappuccino at Dean and Deluca (▷ 77) amid Georgetowners shopping for gourmet treats.

Check out vintage home furnishings in the fun showroom that is Miss Pixie's (▷ 91) on 14th Street.

The popular Dean and Deluca in Georgetown (right)

Washington by Area

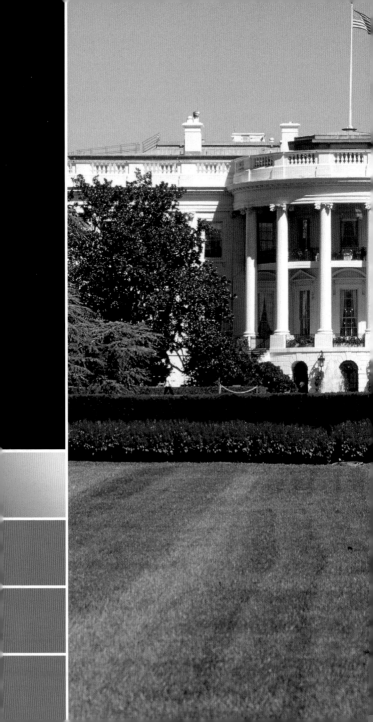

Downtown

This area, stretching west from Chinatown to the White House, has boomed in the last few years and is the city's nerve center. The district is especially popular at night.

MASSACHUSETTS ISLAND AVENUE

O Street

NEW HAMPSHIRE AVENUE

CONNECTICUT

N Street

Jefferson Place

St Matthews Cathedral

RHODE

Scott Circle

N Street

STREET

Avenue

Thomas Circle

13TH STREET

M STREET

Jewish Museum

M Street

Street

Explorers Hall

DeSales Street

AVENUE

National Geographic Museum

14TH

Street

Vermont

L Street

Street

16TH

15th

Street

DOWNTOWN

Farragut North

K STREET

STREET

Franklin Park

K STREET

20th Street

19th Street

18th Street

17th Street

Street

Street

I STREET

Street

Farragut West

St Johns Church

McPherson Square

Street

PENNSYLVANIA AVENUE

H STREET

H STREET

YORK

Renwick Gallery

NEW

15th

14TH

13TH

G Street

Street

The White House

F Street

National Theatre

Warner Theatre

E STREET

E STREET

20TH

VIRGINIA

19th Street

18th Street

D Street

DAR Museum

The Ellipse

C Street

0   250 m
0   250 yds

3

4

5

6

7

E

F

G

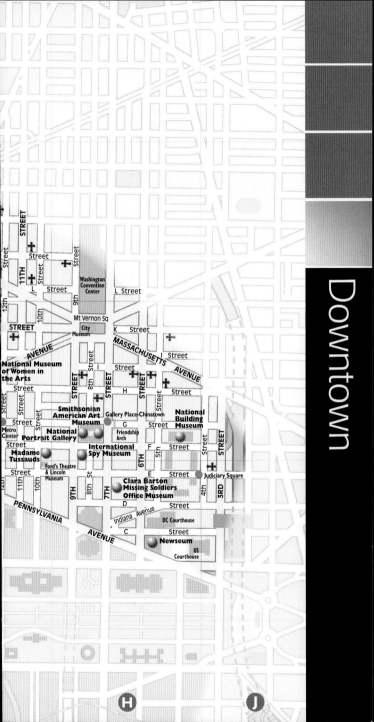

STREET

11TH
Street

Street

Street

Street
L Street

12th

10th

Washington
Convention
Center

9th
Street

L Street

Mt Vernon Sq

STREET

City
Museum

K Street

AVENUE

MASSACHUSETTS

I Street

National Museum
of Women in
the Arts

8th Street

I Street

STREET

AVENUE

H Street

Street

Street

STREET

STREET

7th Street

6TH

Street

H Street

Street

Smithsonian
American Art
Museum

Gallery Place-Chinatown

G Street

National
Building
Museum

STREET

STREET

National
Portrait Gallery

Friendship
Arch

Street

Metro
Center

Street

International
Spy Museum

F Street

5th Street

4th Street

3RD

Madame
Tussauds

6TH

F Street

E Street

Judiciary Square

12th
11th
10th

Street

Ford's Theatre
& Lincoln
Museum

8th St

7TH

Clara Barton
Missing Soldiers
Office Museum

E Street

Street

PENNSYLVANIA

9th Street

D Street

Indiana Avenue

DC Courthouse

AVENUE

C Street

Street

Newseum

US
Courthouse

H

J

International Spy Museum

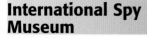

TOP 25

The International Spy Museum illustrates the work of famous spies and explains the role of espionage

THE BASICS

spymuseum.org

✚ H5

✉ 800 F Street NW

☎ 202/393-7798

🕐 Times vary according to the date, so check online

💰 Expensive

♿ Excellent

Ⓜ Gallery Place–Chinatown

HIGHLIGHTS

● Interactive spy experiences
● Exquisitely Evil: 50 Years of Bond Villains

The International Spy Museum has the largest collection of espionage artifacts ever placed on public display. Plan to spend at least two hours and don't miss the entire floor dedicated to James Bond.

Spies throughout history This is the place of dreams for anyone who's ever secretly wished they could cut it as a spy. Hundreds of historic artifacts, photographs, films and videos recall the most famous espionage events in history—from the Greek and Roman empires to the British Empire, both World Wars and, of course, the Cold War. Visitors receive a cover identity when they enter and learn about the tradecraft and tools of spying through the ages, watch films about real spies, and find out about the challenges facing today's spies.

Role playing The immersive interactive experience, Operation Spy, lets visitors play spy for an hour. The aim is to try to complete a mission to intercept a secret weapons deal involving a nuclear device (for over 12s only). The interactive exhibit, Exquisitely Evil: 50 Years of Bond Villains, celebrates the most famous spy of all times, James Bond. The exhibit focuses on Bond's best-known adversaries, from Dr. No to Auric Goldfinger, and looks at how the films were inspired by the threats the world was facing when they were made. For an extra charge you can take part in Spy in the City, a game the museum runs in and around the neighborhood of Downtown DC.

1600 Pennsylvania Avenue, the White House, first occupied by John Adams in 1800

The White House

nps.gov/whho
whitehouse.gov

🔲 F5

✉ 1600 Pennsylvania Avenue

☎ 202/456-7041

🕐 Tours by arrangement only, Tue–Sat

✋ Free

♿ Excellent

Ⓜ McPherson Square, Metro Center

❓ You are required to write to a Member of Congress up to six months in advance to be accepted on a free tour. Foreign visitors should contact their embassy in Washington. For historical exhibits, go to the White House Visitor Center, 1450 Pennsylvania Avenue NW 🕐 Daily 7.30–4 Ⓜ Federal Triangle, Metro Center

In the city's oldest public building, virtually every desk, every sterling tea service, every silver platter, decanter, painting and floor has witnessed historic events of the American democracy.

The President's Palace When he became the second occupant in 1801 of what was then known as the President's Palace, Thomas Jefferson (1743–1826) thought the original design by James Hoban (c. 1762–1831) "big enough for two emperors, one Pope and the grand Lama." Since then the building has had several renovations. The first was necessary after the British burned it in 1814. An almost-complete renovation occurred during the Truman Administration (1945–53) after a piano broke through the floor, and an engineer determined that the building was staying erect only out of "force of habit."

Works of art The president's house holds an impressive display of decorative arts from the Sheraton, French, Queen Anne and Federal periods. There are carved Carrara marble mantels, Bohemian cut-glass chandeliers and Turkish Hereke carpets. The tour may vary depending on official functions, but usually open are the ceremonial East Room, with Gilbert Stuart's 1797 *George Washington* portrait, the Vermeil Room containing 17th- and early 18th-century French and English gilded silver (vermeil), the small drawing room, and the neoclassical State Dining Room where the *Abraham Lincoln* portrait by George P.A. Healy (1813–94) hangs.

● *Abraham Lincoln*, George P.A. Healy
● China Room
● French and English gilded silver
● East Room
● *George Washington*, Gilbert Stuart

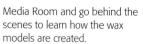

More to See

CLARA BARTON MISSING SOLDIERS OFFICE MUSEUM

clarabartonmuseum.org

Barton's lodgings served as headquarters for her efforts to discover the whereabouts of missing Civil War soldiers.

🔲 H6 ✉ 437 7th Street NW ☎ 202/824-0613 🕐 Thu–Sat 12–7, last admission 6pm, Sun–Wed by appointment 🚇 Gallery Place–Chinatown 💷 Moderate

DAR MUSEUM

dar.org/museum

The National Society of the Daughters of the American Revolution has been collecting pre-Civil War American artifacts for more than 100 years.

🔲 F6 ✉ 1776 D Street NW ☎ 202/628-1776 🕐 Mon–Fri 8.30–4, Sat 9–5 🚇 Farragut West, Farragut North 💷 Free

MADAME TUSSAUDS

madametussauds.com/washington

Take a tour through the glitterati of the world of politics, stage, screen and sport. Be interviewed in the Media Room and go behind the scenes to learn how the wax models are created.

🔲 G5 ✉ 1001 F Street NW ☎ 202/942-7300 🕐 Daily (times vary so check online) 🚇 Metro Center 💷 Expensive

NATIONAL BUILDING MUSEUM

nbm.org

The dramatic interior of this building houses exhibits on DC's cityscape, urban planning and architecture.

🔲 H5 ✉ 401 F Street NW ☎ 202/272-2448 🕐 Mon–Sat 10–5, Sun 11–5 🚇 Judiciary Square 💷 Moderate

NATIONAL GEOGRAPHIC MUSEUM

nationalgeographic.com

Best known for the *National Geographic Magazine*, the Society breathes life into exhibits about the world around us, and has displays of the work of its many talented photographers.

🔲 F4 ✉ 1145 17th Street NW ☎ 202/857-7700 🕐 Daily 10–6 🚇 Farragut West, Farragut North 💷 Expensive

Madame Tussauds

NATIONAL MUSEUM OF WOMEN IN THE ARTS

nmwa.org

The only museum in the US dedicated to the artwork of women, the collection includes around 4,500 objects by 1,000 artists from around the world, from the Renaissance to the present day.

➕ G5 ✉ 1250 New York Avenue NW ☎ 202/783-5000 ⏰ Mon–Sat 10–5, Sun 12–5 🚇 Metro Center 💲 Expensive

NATIONAL PORTRAIT GALLERY

npg.si.edu

This renovated neoclassical gallery has portraits of famous Americans crafted by other famous Americans using visual and performing arts, and new media.

➕ H5 ✉ 8th and F streets NW ☎ 202/633-8300 ⏰ Daily 11.30–7 🚇 Gallery Place–Chinatown 💲 Free

NEWSEUM

newseum.org

This monument to the freedom of the press, with state-of-the-art galleries, has an interactive newsroom and new media gallery.

➕ H6 ✉ 555 Pennsylvania Avenue and 6th Street NW ☎ 202/292-6100 ⏰ Daily 9–5 🚇 Archives–Navy Memorial, Judiciary Square 💲 Expensive

RENWICK GALLERY

americanart.si.edu/renwick

Reopened after a two-year renovation, the Renwick is dedicated to American craft and decorative arts, and hosts temporary exhibits.

➕ F5 ✉ 17th Street NW and Pennsylvania Avenue ☎ 202/633-7970 ⏰ Daily 10–5.30 🚇 Farragut West, Farragut North 💲 Free

SMITHSONIAN AMERICAN ART MUSEUM (SAAM)

americanart.si.edu

The country's first national art collection includes works by Georgia O'Keeffe, Edward Hopper and Roy Lichtenstein, as well as Latino art and photography.

➕ H5 ✉ 8th and F streets NW ☎ 202/633-7970 ⏰ Daily 11.30–7 🚇 Gallery Place–Chinatown 💲 Free

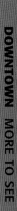

The National Portrait Gallery and Smithsonian American Art Museum

Presidential Route

Presidents parade down Pennsylvania Avenue as part of the inaugural celebrations. Re-enact that procession with this walk.

DISTANCE: 2.25 miles (3.5km) **ALLOW:** 2 hours 45 minutes

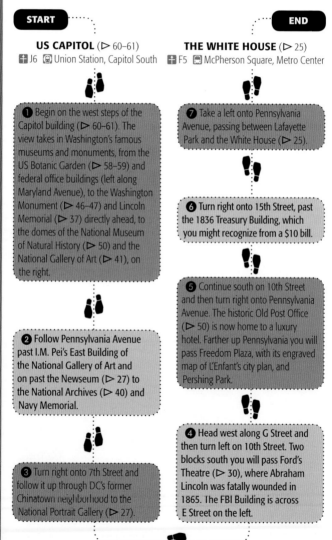

START

US CAPITOL (▷ 60–61)
🚼 J6 🚇 Union Station, Capitol South

END

THE WHITE HOUSE (▷ 25)
🚼 F5 🚇 McPherson Square, Metro Center

❶ Begin on the west steps of the Capitol building (▷ 60–61). The view takes in Washington's famous museums and monuments, from the US Botanic Garden (▷ 58–59) and federal office buildings (left along Maryland Avenue), to the Washington Monument (▷ 46–47) and Lincoln Memorial (▷ 37) directly ahead, to the domes of the National Museum of Natural History (▷ 50) and the National Gallery of Art (▷ 41), on the right.

❷ Follow Pennsylvania Avenue past I.M. Pei's East Building of the National Gallery of Art and on past the Newseum (▷ 27) to the National Archives (▷ 40) and Navy Memorial.

❸ Turn right onto 7th Street and follow it up through DC's former Chinatown neighborhood to the National Portrait Gallery (▷ 27).

❼ Take a left onto Pennsylvania Avenue, passing between Lafayette Park and the White House (▷ 25).

❻ Turn right onto 15th Street, past the 1836 Treasury Building, which you might recognize from a $10 bill.

❺ Continue south on 10th Street and then turn right onto Pennsylvania Avenue. The historic Old Post Office (▷ 50) is now home to a luxury hotel. Farther up Pennsylvania you will pass Freedom Plaza, with its engraved map of L'Enfant's city plan, and Pershing Park.

❹ Head west along G Street and then turn left on 10th Street. Two blocks south you will pass Ford's Theatre (▷ 30), where Abraham Lincoln was fatally wounded in 1865. The FBI Building is across E Street on the left.

Shopping

ALDEN

aldenshoe.com

Alden, originally of New England, sells good quality men's shoes and boots as well as leather accessories.

H5 ✉ 921 F Street NW ☎ 202/347-2308 🕐 Mon–Fri 10–6, Sat 11–5 🚇 Metro Center

CITYCENTERDC

citycenterdc.com/retail

You won't miss the five blocks of luxury shopping and high-end dining in the heart of Downtown. Carolina Herrera, Dior, Tumi and Hermes are here, as well as DC outposts of restaurants Momofuku, Del Frisco's and Mango Tree.

G/H5 ✉ H Street NW and New York Avenue NW ☎ 202/289-9000 🕐 Hours vary 🚇 Metro Center

COUP DE FOUDRE

coupdefoudrelingerie.com

"Love at First Sight" carries high-end European lingerie in its elegant boudoir and offers a fitting service.

G6 ✉ Corner of 11th and E Street NW ☎ 202/393-0878 🕐 Mon–Sat 11–6 🚇 Metro Center

FAHRNEY'S PENS

fahrneyspens.com

This DC institution, started in 1929 by Earl Fahrney, stocks traditional and cutting-edge pens and stationery.

G5 ✉ 1317 F Street NW ☎ 202/628-9525 🕐 Mon–Fri 9.30–6, Sat 10–5 🚇 Metro Center

GALLERY PLACE

galleryplace.com

Gallery Place complex has a movie theater, a bowling alley and retailers like Urban Outfitters.

H5 ✉ 7th and H streets NW 🕐 Hours vary 🚇 Gallery Place–Chinatown

GROOMING LOUNGE

groominglounge.com

The Lounge pampers the modern male with fine grooming and shaving products, shoe shines, shaves and haircuts.

F4 ✉ 1745 L Street NW ☎ 202/466-8900 🕐 Mon–Fri 9–7, Sat 9–6, Sun 10–5.15 🚇 Farragut North, Farragut West

J. PRESS

jpressonline.com

This traditional clothier still strives to "dress men to the Ivy League standard."

F4 ✉ 1801 L Street NW ☎ 202/857-0120 🕐 Mon–Fri 9–6.30, Sat 9.30–6 🚇 Farragut North, Farragut West

NORDSTROM RACK

nordstromrack.com

This popular discount clothing and shoe chain offers high-quality items from Nordstrom's department store at a fraction of the price.

E4 ✉ 18th and L streets NW ☎ 202/627-3650 🕐 Mon–Fri 9–9, Sat 10–9, Sun 11–7 🚇 Farragut West

PROPER TOPPER

propertopper.com

In addition to great hats, charming accessories and home furnishings, you'll find women's and children's wear.

F4 ✉ 1350 Connecticut Avenue NW ☎ 202/842-3055 🕐 Mon–Fri 10–8, Sat 10–6, Sun 11–5 🚇 Dupont Circle

REITER'S BOOKS

reiters.com

Washington's oldest independent bookstore features scientific, technical and professional titles, plus puzzles, games and toys for children of all ages.

E5 ✉ 1900 G Street NW ☎ 202/223-3327 🕐 Mon–Fri 9.30–6, Sat 10–5 🚇 Farragut West

Entertainment and Nightlife

DAR CONSTITUTION HALL

dar.org/constitution-hall

This 3,700-seat hall hosts music, stage shows and comedy acts.

➕ F6 ✉ 18th and C streets NW ☎ 202/628-1776 🚇 Farragut West, then walk six blocks

FORD'S THEATRE

fordstheatre.org

Ford's, where Lincoln was shot, hosts plays and musicals, many for the family.

➕ G5 ✉ 511 10th Street NW ☎ 202/347-4833 🚇 Metro Center

THE HAMILTON

thehamiltondc.com

Classy venue for local blues, swing, R&B and frequent Gospel brunch.

➕ G5 ✉ 600 14th Street NW ☎ 202/787-1000 🕐 Box office opens 5pm on show nights 🚇 Metro Center

POSTE

postebrasserie.com

Poste's patio next to the Hotel Monaco is a great spot to sample the tasty seasonal alcohol infusions.

➕ H5 ✉ 555 8th Street NW ☎ 202/783-6060 🕐 Bar hours: daily from 10.30am (closing times vary) 🚇 Gallery Place–Chinatown

POV ROOF TERRACE

wwashingtondc.com/pov

Take in stunning views while indulging in superb cocktails and light bites.

➕ G5 ✉ 515 15th Street NW ☎ 202/661-2400 🕐 From 3pm Mon–Fri and 11am Sat–Sun (closing times vary) 🚇 McPherson Square

RFD

lovethebeer.com

RFD is frequently packed, with a lively atmosphere and huge beer list.

➕ H5 ✉ 810 7th Street NW ☎ 202/289-2030 🕐 Mon–Thu 11am–2am,

Fri–Sat 11am–3am, Sun 11am–midnight 🚇 Gallery Place–Chinatown

ROUND ROBIN BAR

washington.intercontinental.com

This circular bar maintains the same atmosphere it had in the early 19th century when Senator Henry Clay introduced the bartender to the mint julep.

➕ G6 ✉ 1401 Pennsylvania Avenue NW ☎ 202/628-9100 🕐 Mon–Sat noon–1am, Sun 12–12 🚇 Metro Center

SCIENCE CLUB

scienceclubdc.com

A narrow, multistory lounge with chic decor and DJs in the back room.

➕ E4 ✉ 1136 19th Street NW ☎ 202/775-0747 🕐 Mon–Thu 4.30pm–2am, Fri 4.30pm–3am, Sat 7pm–3am 🚇 Farragut North

SHAKESPEARE THEATRE

shakespearetheatre.org

This theater offers fantastically staged and acted performances of works by the Bard and his contemporaries.

➕ H6 ✉ 450 7th Street NW (Lansburgh Theatre), 610 F Street NW (Sidney Harman Hall) ☎ 202/547-1122 🚇 Gallery Place–Chinatown

VERIZON CENTER

verizoncenter.com

The home of Washington's pro basketball and hockey teams also hosts DC's biggest concerts and the circus.

➕ H5 ✉ 601 F Street NW ☎ 202/628-3200 🚇 Gallery Place–Chinatown

WOOLLY MAMMOTH THEATRE COMPANY

woollymammoth.net

This resident group presents unusual, avant-garde shows in its modern space.

➕ H6 ✉ 641 D Street NW ☎ 202/393-3939 🚇 Gallery Place–Chinatown

Where to Eat

PRICES

Prices are approximate, based on a
3-course meal for one person.
$$$ over $50
$$ $30–$50
$ under $30

BREADLINE ($)

breadline.com

This bakery-café makes everything on
the premises, including the warm rolls,
various sandwiches, salads and home-
made soups.

➕ F5 ✉ 1751 Pennsylvania Avenue NW
☎ 202/822-8900 🕐 Mon–Fri 7–5.30
🚇 Farragut West

CENTRAL ($$$)

centralmichelrichard.com

Michel Richard's award-winning bistro
serves American cuisine with a French
twist. It's very popular so reserve ahead.

➕ G6 ✉ 1001 Pennsylvania Avenue NW
☎ 202/626-0015 🕐 Sun–Fri lunch, Mon–Sat
dinner 🚇 Metro Center

CENTROLINA ($$$)

centrolinadc.com

Fans of chef Amy Brandwein praise her
regional Italian cooking on display here.
There's also a market place to buy
produce and products.

➕ G5 ✉ 974 Palmer Alley NW ☎ 202/898-
2426 🕐 Daily lunch, dinner 🚇 Metro Center

COFFEE CULTURE

The following independent cafés have great
coffee and free WiFi: Tryst (2159 18th Street
NW, 202/232-5500, no WiFi weekends),
Flying Fish Coffee and Tea (3064 Mount
Pleasant Street NW, 202/299-0141) and
Busboys and Poets (2021 14th Street NW
and other locations, 202/387-7638).

CLYDE'S ($$)

clydes.com/gallery-place

There's something for everyone on the
vast American-fare menu in this soaring,
grand saloon and restaurant.

➕ H5 ✉ 707 7th Street NW ☎ 202/349-
3700 🕐 Mon–Thu 11am–2am, Fri 11am–3am,
Sat 10am–3am, Sun 10am–2am 🚇 Gallery
Place–Chinatown

CORDUROY ($$–$$$)

corduroydc.com

You'll find Corduroy in a sleek, two-story
town house, with classy American fare
emphasizing seasonal ingredients.

➕ H4 ✉ 1122 9th Street NW ☎ 202/589-
0699 🕐 Mon–Sat 5.30–10.30 🚇 Mt Vernon
Square/Convention Center

EQUINOX ($$$)

equinoxrestaurant.com

Chef Todd Gray builds beautiful, regional
dishes, blending American cuisine with
European technique.

➕ F5 ✉ 818 Connecticut Avenue NW
☎ 202/331-8118 🕐 Mon–Fri lunch, daily
dinner 🚇 Farragut West

FIVE GUYS ($)

fiveguys.com

Beef aficionados could spend a lifetime
sampling the thousands of ways to
customize these made-to-order burgers.

➕ H5 ✉ 808 H Street NW (plus seven other
DC locations) ☎ 202/393-2900 🕐 Daily
11am–10pm 🚇 Gallery Place–Chinatown

FOUNDING FARMERS ($$)

wearefoundingfarmers.com

This restaurant serves seasonal food
from farms local and not-so-local.

➕ F5 ✉ 1924 Pennsylvania Avenue NW
☎ 202/822-8783 🕐 Mon–Fri breakfast, lunch,
Sat–Sun brunch, daily dinner 🚇 Farragut West,
Foggy Bottom

GRAFFIATO ($$$)

graffiatodc.com

Italian-inspired pizza, small plates and hand-rolled pastas are served in the large dining room, decorated with an industrial twist.

🚉 H5 ✉ 707 6th Street NW ☎ 202/289-3600 🕐 Sun–Thu 11.30am–10pm, Fri–Sat 11.30am–11pm 🚇 Gallery Place–Chinatown

JALEO ($$)

jaleo.com

A lively tapas restaurant, José Andrés' Jaleo serves up small plates that cater to any craving, whether it be for home-made chorizo or fried squid with aioli.

🚉 H6 ✉ 480 7th Street NW ☎ 202/628-7949 🕐 Daily lunch, dinner 🚇 Gallery Place–Chinatown

KELLARI TAVERNA ($$$)

kellaridc.com

Fresh whole fish is the signature offering at this convivial restaurant that pairs seafood with appetizers.

🚉 F5 ✉ 1700 K Street NW ☎ 202/535-5274 🕐 Mon–Sat 11.30–11, Sun 4–10 🚇 Farragut West

MATCHBOX ($$)

matchboxchinatown.com

This warm, stylish pizzeria impresses with wood-oven, gourmet pies and miniburgers, plus a pleasant deck with a fireplace.

🚉 H5 ✉ 713 H Street NW ☎ 202/289-4441 🕐 Daily lunch, dinner 🚇 Gallery Place–Chinatown

NOPA KITCHEN AND BAR ($$)

nopadc.com

An elegant brasserie, nopa focuses on serving American fare with French and Asian influences. The name comes from being North of Pennsylvania Avenue.

🚉 H5 ✉ 800 F Street NW ☎ 202/347-4667 🕐 Sun–Fri lunch, dinner daily 🚇 Gallery Place–Chinatown

OYAMEL ($$$)

oyamel.com

Another of José Andrés' ventures, serving some of the best cocktails in town, solid Oaxacan cuisine and a live, projected view of a Mexican market.

🚉 H6 ✉ 401 7th Street NW ☎ 202/628-1005 🕐 Daily lunch, dinner 🚇 Archives

THE PRIME RIB ($$$)

theprimerib.com

The elegance of a supper club is evoked by live piano music and jackets being required for male patrons. Steakhouse classics such as seafood appetizers, rack of lamb, lobster and a mouthwatering selection of prime steaks continue to draw the city's power brokers.

🚉 E5 ✉ 2020 K Street NW ☎ 202/466-8811 🕐 Mon–Fri 11.30–3, 5–10.30, Sat 5–10.30 🚇 Farragut West

RASIKA ($$–$$$)

rasikarestaurant.com

One of the city's top Indian restaurants, Rasika showcases *tawa* (griddle), *sigri* (open barbecue), tandoori and regional dishes, as well as small plates.

🚉 H6 ✉ 633 D Street NW ☎ 202/637-1222 🕐 Mon–Fri lunch, Mon–Sat dinner 🚇 Archives–Navy Memorial

ZAYTINYA ($$)

zaytinya.com

This Mediterranean *meze* spot is popular for its creative cocktails and inventive Turkish, Greek and Lebanese cuisine.

🚉 H5 ✉ 701 9th Street NW ☎ 202/638-0800 🕐 Daily lunch, dinner 🚇 Gallery Place–Chinatown

Explore the grassy promenade from the Capitol to the Washington Monument.

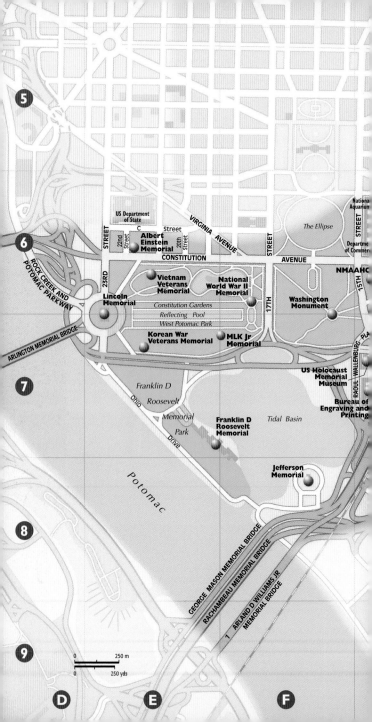

5

6

US Department
of State

22nd Street

23RD Street

C Street

Albert Einstein Memorial

20th Street

VIRGINIA AVENUE

STREET

CONSTITUTION AVENUE

The Ellipse

National Aquarium

STREET

15TH

Departme of Commerc

ROCK CREEK AND POTOMAC PARKWAY

Lincoln Memorial

Vietnam Veterans Memorial

Constitution Gardens

Reflecting Pool

West Potomac Park

Korean War Veterans Memorial

National World War II Memorial

17TH

MLK Jr Memorial

NMAAHC

Washington Monument

ARLINGTON MEMORIAL BRIDGE

7

Franklin D

Roosevelt

Ohio

Memorial

Park

Drive

Franklin D Roosevelt Memorial

Tidal Basin

RAOUL WALLENBURG PLA

US Holocaust Memorial Museum

Bureau of Engraving and Printing

Potomac

Jefferson Memorial

8

GEORGE MASON MEMORIAL BRIDGE

RACHAMBEAU MEMORIAL BRIDGE

1 ARLAND D WILLIAMS JR MEMORIAL BRIDGE

9

0   250 m

0   250 yds

D   **E**   **F**

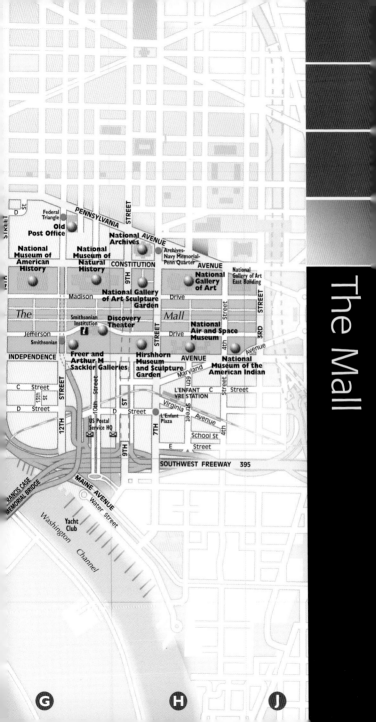

The Mall

D St
Federal
Triangle
Old
Post Office
PENNSYLVANIA AVENUE
National
Archives
Archives-
Navy Memorial-
Penn Quarter
National
Museum of
American
History
National
Museum of
Natural
History
CONSTITUTION AVENUE
National
Gallery
of Art
National
Gallery of Art
East Building
9TH STREET
Madison
National Gallery
of Art Sculpture
Garden
Drive
3RD STREET
The
Smithsonian
Institution
Discovery
Theater
Mall
National
Air and Space
Museum
4th Street
Jefferson
Drive
Smithsonian
INDEPENDENCE
Freer and
Arthur M
Sackler Galleries
Hirshhorn
Museum
and Sculpture
Garden
AVENUE
National
Museum of the
American Indian
Avenue
Maryland
12TH STREET
10th Street
C Street
13th St
D Street
US Postal
Service HQ
9TH STREET
D
Street
ST
7TH STREET
L'ENFANT
VRE STATION
C Street
6th Street
4th Street
Virginia
Avenue
L'Enfant
Plaza
School St
E
Street
SOUTHWEST FREEWAY 395
FRANCIS CASE
MEMORIAL BRIDGE
MAINE AVENUE
Water Street
Yacht
Club
Washington Channel

G H J

FDR and Jefferson Memorials

Bronze statue of Thomas Jefferson (left); the Tidal Basin (right)

THE BASICS

Jefferson Memorial

nps.gov/thje

➕ F8

✉ West Potomac Park, Tidal Basin, south bank

☎ 202/426-6841

🕐 Daily 24 hours. Rangers available to answer questions daily 9.30am–11.30pm 💲 Free

♿ Excellent

🚇 Smithsonian, then 15-min walk

FDR Memorial

nps.gov/frde

➕ E7

✉ West Potomac Park, Tidal Basin, west bank

☎ 202/426-6841

🕐 As for Jefferson above

💲 Free 🚇 Smithsonian, then 10- to 15-min walk

HIGHLIGHTS

● Jefferson bronze
● Inscribed Declaration of Independence
● Wheelchair statue of FDR
● Surrounding cherry trees
● Boat rides in the Tidal Basin

The Jefferson Memorial was dedicated by President Franklin Delano Roosevelt on the 200th anniversary of Jefferson's birth, April 13, 1943. Roosevelt's own memorial was created nearby and dedicated in 1997.

Classical The contributions of Thomas Jefferson, a brilliant statesman and America's third president, are commemorated in a white-marble, neoclassical memorial along Washington's Tidal Basin amid 3,800 Japanese cherry trees. The Memorial was modeled by architect John Russell Pope (1874–1937) on buildings that Jefferson had designed himself at his own home and the University of Virginia, which, in turn, showed deference to the Pantheon in Rome. The open interior of the building has a 19ft (5.8m) bronze of Jefferson, circled by excerpts of his speeches and writings inscribed into the walls. An inscription above Jefferson reads, "I have sworn upon the altar of God eternal hostility against every form of tyranny over the mind of man."

Sculpture Franklin Delano Roosevelt (1882–1945), America's president from the Great Depression through the end of World War II, is memorialized by a park on the west side of the Tidal Basin. The Memorial, cloaked in shady trees amid waterfalls and pools, is divided into four outdoor "rooms," each commemorating one of FDR's four terms in office. Nine sets of bronze sculptures, one of which is a depiction of FDR in a wheelchair, punctuate the park.

Lincoln Memorial

Washington Monument (left); sculpture of Lincoln (middle); the Lincoln Memorial (right)

This powerful and majestic memorial honors the president who led the country through the Civil War and whose legacy gave rise to America's modern civil rights movement. The view from the steps at sunset is one of the city's most inspiring, with the Washington Monument reflected in the rectangular pool at its base.

Tribute Architect Henry Bacon (1866–1924) chose a Greek Doric style for Lincoln's memorial because he felt that a memorial to a man who had sacrificed so much to defend democracy should be modeled after the style found in the birthplace of democracy. Construction, during World War I, was not without difficulties. The marsh-like site required the builders to dig down almost 65ft (20m) to find a suitable foundation. Almost 38,000 tons of material was transported from as far away as Colorado.

History in stone Bacon's white marble temple to Lincoln contains a 19ft (6m) seated statue of the president by Daniel Chester French (1850–1931). The statue was so large that it had to be constructed inside the memorial. The chamber is flanked by two smaller rooms, which contain inscriptions of Lincoln's Gettysburg and second inaugural addresses and two beautiful murals. The area surrounding the Reflecting Pool that stretches east from the foot of the monument has hosted seminal events in America's history, most notably Martin Luther King, Jr.'s "I Have a Dream" speech.

THE BASICS

nps.gov/linc

🔢 E6

✉ 23rd Street NW between Constitution and Independence avenues (west end of the Mall)

☎ 202/426-6841

🕐 As for Jefferson Memorial (▷ 36)

✋ Free

♿ Excellent

Ⓜ Foggy Bottom–GWU

HIGHLIGHTS

● Daniel Chester French's *Lincoln*

● Inscriptions of Lincoln's 1863 Gettysburg Address and Second Inaugural Address

● Reflecting Pool

● View at sunset

Martin Luther King, Jr. Memorial

TOP 25

The impressive statue of Martin Luther King, Jr. stands 29.5ft (9m) high and is the centerpiece of the memorial

THE BASICS

nps.gov/mlkm

🔲 E7

✉ 1964 Independence Avenue SW

☎ 202/426-6841

🕐 As for Jefferson Memorial (▷ 36)

🎫 Free

♿ Excellent

🚇 Smithsonian, then a 10- to 15-min walk

❓ The memorial is located at the northwest corner of the Tidal Basin near the Franklin Delano Roosevelt Memorial

HIGHLIGHTS

● The Mountain of Despair
● The Stone of Hope
● Inscription wall with famous speech passages
● 29.5ft (9m) high stone relief of Dr. King

Visitors to the Martin Luther King, Jr. Memorial take the same symbolic journey that the famous civil rights leader took— they pass through a boulder that has been split in two and named "Mountain of Despair" and emerge at the "Stone of Hope," a reference to his famous speech.

Years of planning It took more than two decades of planning and fundraising to establish this memorial to the famous American civil rights leader, Martin Luther King, Jr. (1929–68), who followed Gandhi's philosophy of peaceful protest. The address of the white granite memorial, which was dedicated on October 16, 2011, is 1964 Independence Avenue SW, in commemoration of the year the Civil Rights Act of 1964 became law.

A symbolic struggle The key message, and symbol, of the memorial is a line from King's "I Have a Dream" speech, which he delivered on the steps of the Lincoln Memorial in 1963: "Out of a mountain of despair, a stone of hope." Harry E. Johnson, president of the Memorial Project Foundation, said the 4-acre (1.5ha) site was "envisioned as a quiet and peaceful space, yet drawing from Dr. King's speeches and using his own rich language, the King Memorial will almost certainly change the heart of every person who visits…a public sanctuary where future generations of Americans, regardless of race, religion, gender, ethnicity or sexual orientation, can come to honor Dr. King."

The Apollo lunar rover (right) and space rockets (left) at the National Air and Space Museum

National Air and Space Museum

One of the most visited museums on the Mall takes you on a pioneering journey from the first manned motorized flight to the most recent space exploration.

Flight pioneers The Smithsonian's bicentennial gift to the nation, this museum receives almost 9 million visitors a year in its monumental glass-and-granite galleries. The collection—begun as early as 1861, when the first secretary of the Smithsonian urged experiments in balloon flight—includes the Wright brothers' 1903 *Flyer*, Charles Lindbergh's *Spirit of St. Louis*, Chuck Yeager's *Bell X-1*, in which he broke the sound barrier, and *The Voyager*, the plane in which Dick Rutan and Jeana Yeager flew nonstop around the world in 1986.

Into space Visitors can touch a moon rock and see the *Apollo 11* and Skylab command modules, and the *Discovery* Space Shuttle. Aside from the Boeing Milestones of Flight Hall, there's exhibits on the space race between the United States and the Soviet Union, exploration of our solar system and the science of flight, among many others. Visitors who tire of the museum's colossal collection can take in an IMAX film, go for a test run in a flight simulator, or visit the Albert Einstein Planetarium and discover the universe. Despite its huge size, the building can only hold about 10 percent of the museum's collection. Most of the rest is housed in hangars at the Steven F. Udvar-Hazy Center near Dulles International Airport.

THE BASICS

airandspace.si.edu

✚ H7

✉ Independence Avenue at 6th Street SW

☎ 202/633-2214

🕐 Daily 10–5.30

💲 Free. Albert Einstein Planetarium: moderate

♿ Excellent

🍴 Wright Place Food Court

🚇 L'Enfant Plaza, Smithsonian

❓ Lockheed Martin IMAX, Udvar-Hazy IMAX: call for schedules. Tours daily

HIGHLIGHTS

● Wright brothers' *Flyer*
● Charles Lindbergh's *Spirit of St. Louis*
● Chuck Yeager's *Bell X-1 Glamorous Glennis*
● The Steven F. Udvar-Hazy Center
● John Glenn's *Friendship* and *Apollo 11*
● *Discovery* Space Shuttle
● Skylab Command Module
● Lunar exploration vehicles

THE MALL TOP 25

National Archives

The National Archives (left); inspecting the Archives' historic documents (right)

THE BASICS

archives.gov

🚻 H6

✉ Constitution Avenue at 7th Street NW

☎ 877/444-6777

🕐 Daily 10–5.30

🎫 Free

♿ Excellent

🚇 Archives–Navy Memorial

❓ Guided tours Mon–Fri 9.45am (reservations required)

HIGHLIGHTS

● Charters of Freedom
● Murals by Barry Faulkner
● Changing exhibition gallery

Behind this building's colossal bronze doors, America's story comes alive through millions of items, including the founding documents, the rifle used to shoot John F. Kennedy (1917–63) and the Watergate tapes.

Charters of Freedom Under low light in the magnificent central rotunda lie 14 of America's founding documents, including the Constitution, the Declaration of Independence and the Bill of Rights. All have been encased in state-of-the-art, gold-plated, titanium frames filled with inert argon gas. Two 340lb (154kg) murals, *The Constitution* and *The Declaration of Independence*, accentuate the experience.

Archival splendor The Archives is most famous for the Charters of Freedom, but this building contains billions of other documents, maps and photographs, plus hundreds of thousands of miles of film and videotapes, the most entertaining and instructional of which are on display in the Public Vaults. This child-friendly area showcases audio recordings of congressional debates on prohibition, video clips of former presidents cracking jokes and behind-the-scenes conversations between President Kennedy and his advisors during the Cuban Missile Crisis, among many other exhibits, all displayed in accessible multimedia presentations. The William G. McGowan Theater screens films about the Archives and the Charters of Freedom by day and documentary films at night.

National Gallery of Art

Monet's Woman with a Parasol *(left); the dome of the main atrium (right)*

Housed in two distinctive buildings, the National Gallery contains one of the world's preeminent collections of paintings, drawings, sculptures and photographs ranging from the Middle Ages to the modern day.

West Building Designed by John Russell Pope in the classical style, this building was funded by a gift from Andrew Mellon, a former treasury secretary. Mellon also donated an impressive collection of art that has been augmented to fill the building's many galleries. Of particular interest are da Vinci's *Ginevra*, works by Vermeer and Monet, and a comprehensive collection of American art. The building is complemented by a large rotunda filled with flowers and the gentle sounds of a fountain, and by small garden courts in each wing of the building. The National Gallery frequently stages some of the nation's finest temporary exhibitions.

East Building This architectural masterpiece was created by I.M. Pei (b.1917), and opened in 1978. The galleries of the East Building, home to the modern art collection, have been undergoing renovations for three years and are now fully open again. The renovations have added new gallery space and a stunning Roof Terrace that features several outdoor sculptures, including *Hahn/Cock* by Katharina Fritsch (a very large, very blue cockerel) on long-term loan. There are two new Tower Galleries, with works by Rothko and Calder.

THE BASICS

nga.gov

🕂 H6

✉ Entrances on the Mall, on 7th Street, Constitution Avenue, 6th Street and 4th Street

☎ 202/737-4215

🕐 Mon–Sat 10–5, Sun 11–6

💷 Free

♿ Excellent

🍴 Cascade Café, Garden Café, Pavilion Café,

🚇 Archives–Navy Memorial, Judiciary, Smithsonian

❓ Tours daily

HIGHLIGHTS

● New East galleries
● *Venus and Adonis*, Titian
● *The Alba Madonna*, Raphael
● *Laocoòn*, El Greco
● *Daniel in the Lions' Den*, Peter Paul Rubens
● *Woman Holding a Balance*, Johannes Vermeer
● *A Girl with a Watering Can*, Auguste Renoir
● *Woman with a Parasol—Madame Monet and her Son*, Claude Monet
● *The Skater*, Gilbert Stuart

HIGHLIGHTS

- Contemplative Court
- The Central Hall
- The reflecting pool
- Views from the museum
- The striking building

This landmark museum, on the Mall next to the Washington Monument, seeks to be a place where visitors can learn about the richness and diversity of the African-American experience, what that experience means to their lives and how it helped shape the United States.

The new museum President George W. Bush signed the legislation establishing the National Museum of African American History and Culture in 2003; the Smithsonian broke ground for the museum in February 2012. The 400,000 sq ft (37,000 sq m) building has five levels above ground and four below housing exhibition galleries, an education center, a theater, café and store, as well as staff offices. A unique feature of the building's design is

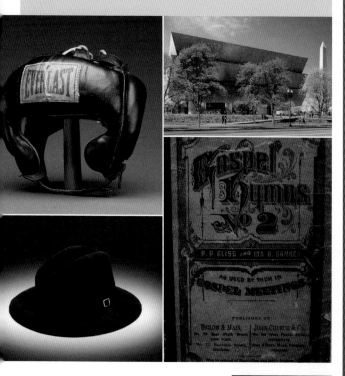

Clockwise from far left: Louis Armstrong's brass-and-gold trumpet, made in 1946; headgear worn by Muhammad Ali when he trained at 5th Street Gym; the new building; Harriet Tubman's hymnal; Michael Jackson's fedora; a cadillac from Chuck Berry's personal fleet

a series of openings—or lenses—throughout the exhibition spaces that frame views of the Washington Monument, the White House and other Smithsonian museums on the Mall. The aim of these framed views is to remind those who visit that the museum presents a view of America through the lens of the African-American experience.

Exhibits The 11 inaugural exhibitions focus on broad themes of history and community. Highlights include: a segregation-era railway car (c. 1920), Nat Turner's Bible (c. 1830s), Michael Jackson's fedora (c. 1992), a slave cabin from Edisto Island, S.C. plantation (early 1800s), Harriet Tubman's hymnal (c. 1876) and works of art by Charles Alston, Elizabeth Catlett, Romare Bearden and Henry O. Tanner.

THE BASICS
nmaahc.si.edu
⊞ G6
✉ Madison Drive NW
☎ 202/633-1000
💵 Free
♿ Excellent
🍴 Café
Ⓜ Smithsonian, Federal Triangle

National Museum of the American Indian

The futuristic exterior (left); traditional shirt (middle); the rotunda display (right)

HIGHLIGHTS

● Limestone exterior and Grandfather Rocks
● Welcome Wall
● *Who We Are* film
● 20ft (6m) totem pole by Nathan Jackson
● Light-filled atrium
● Navajo weavings
● ImagiNATIONS Activity Center

The first national museum dedicated to Native Americans, this Smithsonian building pays homage to thousands of cultures with great cohesion.

Connection to nature The exterior, made out of Minnesota limestone, resembles a weatherworn rock mass, and the building sits on a serene 4.25-acre (1.7ha) plot with fountains and Grandfather Rocks (40 ancient rocks linking the Native American people to the environment). Inside, light is refracted from a prism in the ceiling into the museum's Potomac atrium, which often plays host to traditional ceremonies.

Break from tradition The museum breaks from the traditional anthropological treatment of Native Americans. "Our Universes" explores the spiritual relationship between humans and nature. "Return to a Native Place: Algonquian Peoples of the Chesapeake" informs visitors about the continued Native presence in the region. "Nation to Nation: Treaties between the United States and American Indian Nations" examines the history of US/American Indian diplomacy. The Red Power movement of the 1960s and '70s is also highlighted. A large gallery space showcases the talents of Native American artists. The Lelawi Theater shows a spectacular film, *Who We Are,* to introduce the main themes of the museum. The Rasmuson Theater features storytelling, dance and music.

US Holocaust Memorial Museum

People visit the museum (left) to pay their respects at the displays (middle) and remember the lives lost (right)

This memorial to the millions of Jews and other targeted groups killed by the Nazis between 1933 and 1945 graphically portrays the personal stories and wider issues of persecution and human tragedy. The museum sets new standards for historical interpretation.

Disturbing "You cannot deal with the Holocaust as a reasonable thing," explained architect James Ingo Freed (1930–2005). To that end, he created a discordant building, intended to disturb the classical and some-times placid facades elsewhere in Washington. Likewise, the central atrium, the Hall of Witness, disorients with twisted skylights, exposed load-bearing brick and architectural elements that don't join in conventional ways.

Nightmare Visitors are given identity cards that detail the life of a Holocaust victim as they enter a detailed history of the rise of anti-Semitism in Europe, the Nazi party and the machinations of the Holocaust. The brilliant and shocking dis-plays are rendered using high-tech audiovisuals. Some viewers are moved to tears. The Hall of Remembrance, a place for quiet reflection, is a welcome respite at the end of the experience. A special exhibit for children 8 and over, "Daniel's Story," re-creates what life was like for a young boy trapped in the downward spiral of Nazi occupation. The Wexner Center, which holds temporary exhibitions, embodies the museum's forward-looking efforts to curb genocide.

THE BASICS

ushmm.org

🔸 G7

✉ 100 Wallenberg Place SW, south of Independence Avenue

☎ 202/488-0400

🕐 Daily 10–5.15. Closed Yom Kippur

💵 Free

♿ Excellent

🍴 Vegetarian café

Ⓜ Smithsonian

❓ Mar–Aug free timed tickets distributed from 10am on a first come, first served basis; also available online in advance

HIGHLIGHTS

● Hall of Witness
● Hall of Remembrance
● For children (aged 8 and over): "Daniel's Story"

Washington Monument

HIGHLIGHTS

● Views from the top
● Museum at the 490-foot level

TIPS

● Make reservations online in advance, even during the off season.
● Take a map of the city with you to the top so that you can point out your favorite places.
● Try to go at sunset to see the whole city painted in pastels.

An icon of Washington life, this monolith is the world's tallest masonry structure. The 70-second ride to the top is rewarded with a marvelous panorama over DC, Maryland and Virginia.

Rogues and cattle The Washington National Monument Society was founded in 1833 to solicit designs and funding for a memorial to America's first president. Construction began in 1848 but stopped in 1854 for over 20 years, in part because a rogue political party stole and destroyed a stone donated by the Pope. During this time, herds of Union cattle grazed on the grounds of the half-finished monument. A ring still betrays the slightly different marble that had to be used years later as construction began again amid the fervor

Clockwise from far left: The Stars and Stripes flying in the breeze below the Washington Monument; view from the top of the monument; the obelisk towering over the city of Washington; the monument reflected in the Tidal Basin; the Washington Monument and the Lincoln Memorial at dusk

surrounding the centennial of the American Revolution. In 1884, 36 years after the cornerstone was placed, a 6.28lb (2.85kg) aluminum point, at the time one of the world's most expensive metals, was placed on top of the 555ft (169m) monument, the tallest building in the world at that time.

View The observation deck, which opened in 2002, is 500ft (152m) above the ground. The views from the top cover most of Washington, as well as parts of Maryland and Virginia: look for the Tidal Basin, the Jefferson and Lincoln memorials, the White House, the US Capitol, the Library of Congress and the Smithsonian Institution. There are 193 commemorative stones donated by states, masonic lodges, church groups and foreign countries.

THE BASICS

nps.gov/wamo

➕ F6

✉ The Mall at 15th Street NW

☎ 202/426-6841

🕐 Daily 9–4.45 (until 9.45 Memorial Day to Labor Day)

💵 $1.50 service charge per ticket if booked in advance, otherwise free on first-come, first-served basis. Get there early for timed tickets

♿ Excellent

Ⓜ Smithsonian

Vietnam Veterans Memorial

Glenna Goodacre sculpture (left); names of heroes on the black granite walls (right)

THE BASICS

nps.gov/vive

➕ E6

✉ Near Constitution Avenue between 21st and 22nd streets NW, adjacent to the Lincoln Memorial

☎ 202/426-6841

🕐 Daily 24 hours

💵 Free

♿ Excellent

🚇 Foggy Bottom, then 15-min walk

❓ Rangers available to assist in locating names

HIGHLIGHTS

● Inscribed names
● Frederick Hart's sculptural group
● Glenna Goodacre's sculptural group
● The city reflected in the polished stone

This black granite wall cut into the earth contains the names of service people killed during the Vietnam War. Despite a design process that was fraught with acrimony and misunderstanding (some suggested throwing the design out and starting again), the completed memorial has become one of the most revered sites in Washington.

Simple reminder Yale University student Maya Ying Lin (b.1959) was only 21 when she won the national design competition with a simple memorial—two triangular black granite walls, each 246ft (75m) long, set at a 125-degree angle and pointing toward the Washington Monument and Lincoln Memorial. The walls rise to 10ft (3m), seeming to overpower those who stand below. Names of soldiers who made the ultimate sacrifice for their country are listed chronologically. Between 1959 and 1975 more than 58,000 were killed or reported missing in action. In 1984 Frederick Hart's sculpture, *The Three Servicemen*, was dedicated at the south entrance and in 1993 the *Vietnam Women's Memorial* by Glenna Goodacre was unveiled.

A place to reflect The polished surface reflects sky, trees, nearby monuments and the faces of visitors searching for the names of loved ones. Each day NPS Rangers collect mementoes left near soldiers' names and carefully place them in storage. Some are on display at the National Museum of American History (▷ 50).

More to See

ALBERT EINSTEIN MEMORIAL

This bronze of Einstein, in a shaded elm grove at the National Academy of Sciences, is an urban oasis.
➕ E6 ✉ Constitution Avenue and 22nd Street NW 🕐 Mon–Fri 9–5 🚇 Foggy Bottom, then 15-min walk 🎟 Free access

BUREAU OF ENGRAVING AND PRINTING

moneyfactory.gov
Watch the powerful printing presses turn out millions of dollars every day.
➕ G7 ✉ 14 and C streets SW ☎ 866/874-2330 🕐 Visitor Center: Sep–Feb Mon–Fri 8.30–3.30; Mar–Aug 8.30–6.30 🚇 Smithsonian 🎟 Free but tickets required Mar–Aug. Booth on Raoul Wallenberg Place ❓ Tours every 15 min Sep–Feb 9–10.45, 12.30–2; Mar–Aug 9–10.45, 12.30–3.45, 5–6

DISCOVERY THEATER

discoverytheater.org
Smithsonian shows here include puppetry, music and storytelling.
➕ G7 ✉ 1100 Jefferson Drive SW ☎ 200/633-8700 🕐 Check online for schedule 🚇 Smithsonian 🎟 Inexpensive

The Korean War Veterans Memorial

FREER GALLERY OF ART AND ARTHUR M. SACKLER GALLERY

asia.si.edu
Connected by an underground passageway, these two museums represent the national museum of Asian art for the United States. In addition, the Freer Gallery contains an important collection of 19th-century American art.
➕ G7 ✉ 1050 Independence Avenue SW ☎ 202/633-1000 🕐 Daily 10–5.30 🚇 Smithsonian 🎟 Free ❓ The Freer is closed until 2017, but the Sackler is open

HIRSHHORN MUSEUM AND SCULPTURE GARDEN

hirshhorn.si.edu
This gallery showcases some first-rate art, including works by Henri Matisse, Man Ray and Andy Warhol.
➕ H7 ✉ 7th Street and Independence Avenue SW ☎ 202/633-4674 🕐 Daily 10–5.30, garden 7.30am–dusk 🚇 L'Enfant Plaza 🎟 Free

KOREAN WAR VETERANS MEMORIAL

nps.gov/kowa
This memorial depicts 19 life-size figures marching through rugged terrain toward an American flag. The faces of 2,400 servicemen are etched into a wall nearby.
➕ E7 ✉ Adjacent to Lincoln Memorial ☎ 202/426-6841 🕐 Daily 24 hours 🚇 Foggy Bottom 🎟 Free

NATIONAL GALLERY OF ART SCULPTURE GARDEN

nga.gov
Many works by Bourgeois, Miró, Lichtenstein and other 20th-century sculptors are on display in this garden, which is set around a fountain

that transforms into a very popular ice rink in winter.

✚ H6 ✉ Between Constitution Avenue and the Mall, 7th and 9th streets NW ☎ 202/737-4215 🕐 Mon–Sat 10–5, Sun 11–6. Skating rink: winter daily, hours vary 🍴 Pavilion Café 🚇 Archives–Navy Memorial 💷 Free. Skating moderate

NATIONAL MUSEUM OF AMERICAN HISTORY

americanhistory.si.edu

From Seinfeld's puffy shirt to ballgowns of the First Ladies, this museum, currently being renovated one gallery at a time, is where you can find America's mementoes.

✚ G6 ✉ Constitution Avenue and 14th Street NW ☎ 202/633-1000 🕐 Daily 10–5.30 🚇 Smithsonian, Federal Triangle 💷 Free ❓ Tours

NATIONAL MUSEUM OF NATURAL HISTORY

mnh.si.edu

Dinosaurs, the Hope Diamond, fossils and millions of plant and animal specimens are all housed here.

✚ G6 ✉ Constitution Avenue and 10th Street NW ☎ 202/633-1000 🕐 Daily 10–5.30 🚇 Smithsonian, Federal Triangle 💷 Free

NATIONAL WORLD WAR II MEMORIAL

nps.gov/nwwm

This oval memorial commemorates the sacrifices made by Americans during World War II.

✚ F6 ✉ The Mall at 17th Street SW ☎ 202/426-6841 🕐 Daily 24 hours 🚇 Smithsonian, then 10-min walk 💷 Free

OLD POST OFFICE BUILDING TOWER

nps.gov/opot

The clock tower here offers a dramatic view of the city. The building has been closed while it's renovated into a luxury hotel, but you'll still be able to go up the tower itself.

✚ G6 ✉ Pennsylvania Avenue at 12th Street NW ☎ 202/606-8691 🕐 Opening hours under review 🍴 Many cafés and restaurants 🚇 Federal Triangle 💷 Free

The Old Post Office

Cartoon depicting jazz musician Duke Ellington, displayed in the National Museum of American History

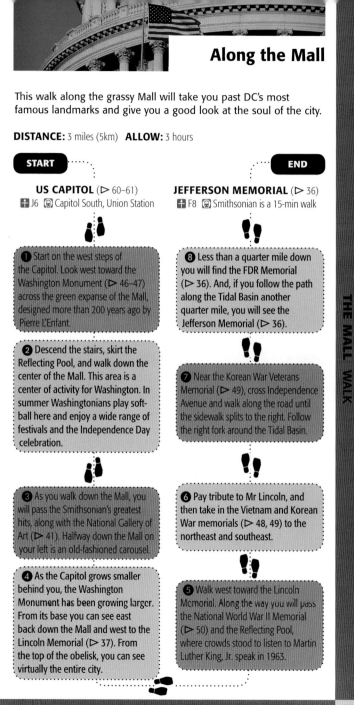

Along the Mall

This walk along the grassy Mall will take you past DC's most famous landmarks and give you a good look at the soul of the city.

DISTANCE: 3 miles (5km)   **ALLOW:** 3 hours

START

US CAPITOL (▷ 60–61)
J6   Capitol South, Union Station

END

JEFFERSON MEMORIAL (▷ 36)
F8   Smithsonian is a 15-min walk

❶ Start on the west steps of the Capitol. Look west toward the Washington Monument (▷ 46–47) across the green expanse of the Mall, designed more than 200 years ago by Pierre L'Enfant.

❷ Descend the stairs, skirt the Reflecting Pool, and walk down the center of the Mall. This area is a center of activity for Washington. In summer Washingtonians play softball here and enjoy a wide range of festivals and the Independence Day celebration.

❸ As you walk down the Mall, you will pass the Smithsonian's greatest hits, along with the National Gallery of Art (▷ 41). Halfway down the Mall on your left is an old-fashioned carousel.

❹ As the Capitol grows smaller behind you, the Washington Monument has been growing larger. From its base you can see east back down the Mall and west to the Lincoln Memorial (▷ 37). From the top of the obelisk, you can see virtually the entire city.

❽ Less than a quarter mile down you will find the FDR Memorial (▷ 36). And, if you follow the path along the Tidal Basin another quarter mile, you will see the Jefferson Memorial (▷ 36).

❼ Near the Korean War Veterans Memorial (▷ 49), cross Independence Avenue and walk along the road until the sidewalk splits to the right. Follow the right fork around the Tidal Basin.

❻ Pay tribute to Mr Lincoln, and then take in the Vietnam and Korean War memorials (▷ 48, 49) to the northeast and southeast.

❺ Walk west toward the Lincoln Memorial. Along the way you will pass the National World War II Memorial (▷ 50) and the Reflecting Pool, where crowds stood to listen to Martin Luther King, Jr. speak in 1963.

THE MALL WALK

51

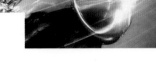

Shopping

NATIONAL AIR AND SPACE MUSEUM
airandspace.si.edu
A three-floor temple to aviation and souvenirs, this gift shop stocks toy rockets, model planes, kites and more.
➕ H7 ✉ Independence Avenue and 4th Street SW ☎ 202/633-2214 🕐 Daily 10–5.30 🚇 L'Enfant Plaza

NATIONAL GALLERY OF ART
nga.gov
In the West Building, this shop carries stationery, prints, scarves and jewelry, along with other items based on the current traveling exhibition.
➕ H6 ✉ 6th Street and Constitution Avenue NW ☎ 202/842-6002 🕐 Mon–Sat 10–5, Sun 11–6 🚇 Archives–Navy Memorial

NATIONAL MUSEUM OF THE AMERICAN INDIAN
nmai.si.edu
This museum's gift shop sells high-grade textiles, jewelry and crafts made by Native American artisans.
➕ H7 ✉ 4th Street SW and Independence Avenue ☎ 202/633-7030 🕐 Daily 10–5.30 🚇 L'Enfant Plaza

NATIONAL MUSEUM OF NATURAL HISTORY
mnh.si.edu
Five separate gift shops at this museum stock items ranging from dinosaur skeleton model kits to well-made jewelry.
➕ G6 ✉ Constitution Avenue and 10th Street NW ☎ 202/633-2060 🕐 Daily 10–5.30 🚇 Smithsonian

Where to Eat

PRICES
Prices are approximate, based on a 3-course meal for one person.
$$$ over $50
$$ $30–$50
$ under $30

MASALA ART ($$)
masalaartdc.com
Flavors of Northern India come to life in the tandoori and *tawa* dishes that appeal to both vegetarians and meat eaters. A pre-theater menu and weekend brunch make this light-filled dining room worth visiting any day of the week.
➕ H8 ✉ 1101 4th Street SW ☎ 202/554-1101 🕐 Mon–Sat 11–2.30, Sun–Thu 5–10, Fri–Sat 5–10.30pm 🚇 Waterfront

MUZE ($$$)
mandarinoriental.com/washington
Enjoy waterside views and a relaxed atmosphere at this stylish restaurant that serves international cuisine with the flavor of Southeast Asia.
➕ H7 ✉ 1330 Maryland Avenue SW ☎ 202/787-6148 🕐 Daily 11.30–4, 5.30–10 🚇 Smithsonian, then 10-min walk

PAVILION CAFÉ ($)
pavilioncafe.com
Inside the National Gallery of Art Sculpture Garden, Pavilion serves up tasty paninis, wraps and salads.
➕ H6 ✉ Entrance via Constitution Avenue and Madison Drive at 9th Street NW ☎ 202/289-3361 🕐 Mon–Thu 10–7, Fri–Sat 10–9, Sun 11–7 🚇 Archives–Navy Memorial

Dominated by federal buildings, Capitol Hill is home to the Capitol building, Union Station, the Supreme Court and the Library of Congress. Neighborhoods of Victorian houses stretch east from these buildings.

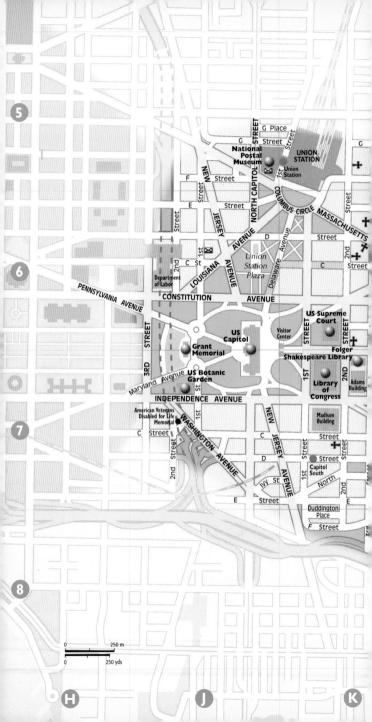

Street

Morris
Place

F
Groff
Court
Street

E
4th Street
5th Street
6th Street

Acker Place
Street

MARYLAND AVENUE
8TH STREET

Lexington
Place
Street
7th Street
9th Street
10th Street
11th Street
Street

D
Street
Street
C

AVENUE
Street
Street

Stanton
Park

CONSTITUTION
Frederick
Douglass Museum
A
Street
Street

Park
Street
12th Place

Street

12th Street
AVENUE

Tennessee Avenue

CAPITOL
HILL
EAST
CAPITOL STREET

Lincoln
Park
Emancipation
Memorial

Street
Street
7th Street
9th Street

A
Street
4th Street
5th Street
6th Street

Street
7th Street

INDEPENDENCE
AVENUE
Street
STREET
Street
Street
Walter
Street
13th Street

Seward
Avenue
Eastern
Market
Massachusetts Avenue

Carolina
Square
C
Street
STREET
Street
Street
South Carolina Avenue
12th Street

Street
Eastern Market
Street
D
11TH STREET
Street

D
Street
Street
Street
PENNSYLVANIA AVENUE
Street
South Carolina

E
Street
4th Street
5th Street
6th Street
Street
8TH STREET
9th Street
10th Street
Street
G
Street

L   M

Library interior (left);
the Torch of Learning
on top of the dome
(below); Library of
Congress (right)

TOP 25

Library of Congress

One of the world's largest libraries, the
de facto national library contains more
than 158 million items, in 470 languages,
on 530 miles (853km) of shelves. It wel-
comes scholars, the general public and,
of course, Congress. The interiors of the
main Jefferson Building are as ornate as
their exterior would suggest.

A universal approach Congress appropriated
funds for a library in 1800, but it was destroyed
by the British when they burned the Capitol
in 1814. Thomas Jefferson's personal library,
one of the finest in the world, then became
the nucleus of the new collection. Jefferson's
approach to knowledge and book collection
became the philosophy for the library itself,
despite its intended purpose to be a resource
for congresspeople and their staff. The library
now files more than 12,000 new books a day,
all copyrighted in the US. The library has also
collected random historical items including the
contents of Lincoln's pockets on the evening he
was shot, and original scores by Beethoven.

Room to read The Italian Renaissance
Jefferson Building houses the library's Main
Reading Room. A dozen figures representing
the countries or empires that were pivotal in the
creation of Western civilization look down from
the apex of the 160ft (49m) dome. It is sup-
ported by columns topped by female figures
representing aspects of civilized life, including
religion, commerce, history and art.

THE BASICS

loc.gov

✚ K7

✉ 1st Street and
Independence Avenue SE

☎ 202/707-5000

🕐 Mon–Sat 8.30–5

💰 Free

♿ Excellent. Visitor
Services (☎ 202/707-
9779) has American Sign
Language interpretation

🍴 Cafeteria, coffee shop,
snack bars

Ⓜ Capitol South

❓ Tours begin at the
Jefferson Building Mon–
Sat 10.30, 11.30, 12.30,
1.30, 2.30, 3.30 (Sat no
12.30 and 3.30 tours).
Resources are open to
over-16s pursuing research

HIGHLIGHTS

● Torch of Learning on
green copper dome
● Beaux Arts design
● Main Reading Room
● Sculpture inside and out
● View of the Capitol from
the Madison Building
cafeteria

US Botanic Garden

HIGHLIGHTS

● Seasonal displays
● Orchids and tropical plants
● Coffee, chocolate and banyan trees
● Bartholdi Fountain

TIP

● Make sure you wear layers as the temperatures in the glasshouse's rooms are set to suit the plants, not necessarily you.

A microcosm of climates in the US, the Botanic Garden lets you experience the desert of Arizona even when it's cold out. Blooms flower all year and December's poinsettia display is a crowd pleaser.

Exotic glasshouse plants In 1838, Congress authorized Lieutenant Charles Wilkes—a surly captain said to be the inspiration for Melville's Captain Ahab—and his crew to circle the globe so that they might provide more accurate charts for the whaling industry. Wilkes returned in 1842 with a collection of exotic plant species, and Congress rekindled dormant plans for a botanical garden. The present conservatory, an attractive combination of iron-and-glass greenhouse and stone orangeries, was erected in 1933. Following a four-year, $33.5 million

A tall cactus in the massive glasshouse at the US Botanic Garden (left); a tranquil escape from the crowds on the Mall, the Conservatory houses lush tropical plants and trees (right)

renovation project, the garden is now home to more than 65,000 plants.

Flowers for all seasons The main entrance hall serves as a seasonal gallery displaying by turns Christmas poinsettias, tulips and hyacinths or chrysanthemums. The conservatory's 14 viewing areas feature plants grown for different uses and in different environments—from high desert flora to the jungle and from coffee and chocolate trees to plants that help us fight cancer. Tucked in the gardens are four specimens—the Vessel Fern, the Ferocious Blue Cycad and two Sago Palms—that are believed to be directly related to those brought back on the Wilkes expedition. The fountain in the adjacent Bartholdi Park was sculpted by Frederic Bartholdi, designer of the Statue of Liberty.

THE BASICS

usbg.gov

🔢 J7

✉ 1st Street SW and Independence Avenue (100 Maryland Avenue SW)

☎ 202/225-8333

🕐 Conservatory and National Garden daily 10–5. Bartholdi Park dawn to dusk

💷 Free

♿ Excellent

🚇 Federal Center

US Capitol

HIGHLIGHTS

● Rotunda
● Frescoes by Constantino Brumidi
● Paintings by John Trumbull
● Visit to the House or Senate Chambers (not part of the Capitol tour—separate pass required)

TIP

● Be aware that the dome is undergoing restoration and is partially obscured. Work should be completed by the 2017 inauguration.

The US Capitol has stood on this hillside since the federal government came to the city in 1800. It is here that members of Congress go about their law-making work—a state-of-the-art visitor center explains this work and more.

Icon The 4,500-ton, cast-iron dome was an engineering feat when undertaken in 1851 by Capitol architect Thomas U. Walter and US Army Captain Montgomery Meigs. It became a political symbol before it was even half finished: the Civil War broke out while it was under construction, and the Capitol housed the wounded. Many advised President Lincoln to halt work on the building, but he was adamant that progress continue as "a sign we intend the Union shall go on." The dome was completed in 1868.

Clockwise from far left: The famous dome of the US Capitol; visitors inspecting the Rotunda; the Capitol is visible from nearly every part of the city, as it stands at the very heart of Washington; the columns of the Capitol; classical figures adorning the Capitol's exterior

THE BASICS

visitthecapitol.gov

✚ J6

✉ East Capitol and 1st Street

☎ 202/226-8000

🕐 Mon–Sat 8.30–4.30

💷 Free

♿ Excellent

🍴 Restaurant

🚇 Capitol South, Union Station, Federal Center

❓ Tours run Mon–Sat 8.50–3.10 and are free but require passes. US citizens can ask their elected representatives; anyone can book online. A limited number of same-day passes are available daily at the information desks at the Visitor Center. Don't bring large bags such as backpacks, as they are prohibited

Founding Fathers Visitors to the Capitol can tour the old Supreme Court Chamber where famous cases have been decided; Statuary Hall, where the House of Representatives first met; the old Senate Chamber, where Webster, Clay and Calhoun famously sparred; and the ornate Brumidi Corridors (special tour Mon–Fri 2pm). But the crowning moment of the tour is the Rotunda, under the Capitol dome. Eight gigantic murals, four by George Washington's aide John Trumbull, depict scenes from the colonies and the revolutionary period. *The Apotheosis of Washington*, visible through the eye of the inner dome, depicts classical deities surrounding the first president. Constantino Brumidi (1805–80), who painted the fresco, was said to consort with prostitutes whose likenesses then appeared in the painting.

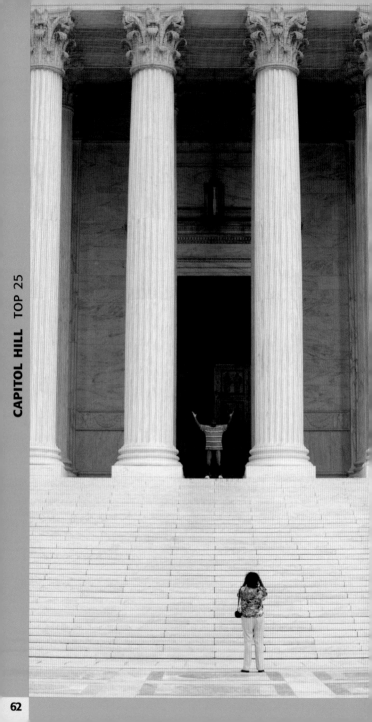

US Supreme Court Building

Exterior of the US Supreme Court (left and below); detail of Contemplation of Justice *(right)*

The home of the highest judicial body in the United States, the Supreme Court, was not constructed here until 1935. Architect Cass Gilbert appears as a member of the sculpture group in the pediment over the entrance.

Judgments The Court considers only cases that have far-reaching implications. The 1857 Dred Scott decision, which held that Congress had no authority to limit slavery, contributed to the onset of the Civil War. Rulings on abortion have frequently made the plaza in front of the building a focus of civil disobedience. *Brown v. Board of Education* required the integration of schools and bus travel across the land and in 2015 the Court ruled in favor of same-sex marriage nationwide. Justice Elena Kagan, appointed in 2010, is only the fourth woman to serve on the court in 226 years.

Law in action The steps up to the colonnaded entrance are flanked by two white-marble allegorical figures by James Earle Fraser, depicting *The Contemplation of Justice* and *The Authority of Law*. The magnificent bronze entrance doors lead into an entrance hall adorned with busts of all the former chief justices. When the court is in session you can join the "three-minute line" and glimpse proceedings from the Standing Gallery. A statue of John Marshall, Chief Justice from 1755 to 1835, dominates the street level, where a short film and changing exhibits describe the work of the court.

THE BASICS

supremecourt.gov

✚ K6

✉ 1st and East Capitol streets NE

☎ 202/479-3000

🕐 Mon–Fri 9–5

💵 Free

♿ Excellent

🍴 Cafeteria

🚇 Capitol South, Union Station

❓ Lectures on the half-hour when the court is not in session 9.30–3.30

HIGHLIGHTS

● Bronze entrance doors
● Plaza sculpture
● Busts of chief justices
● Film and exhibits on Court history
● The court in session

More to See

EASTERN MARKET

easternmarket-dc.org

This food market has been in continuous operation since 1873. Local wares and a farmer's market appear outside on the weekend (▷ 66).

🔲 L7 ✉ 225 7th Street SE 🕐 Tue–Fri 7–7, Sat 7–6, Sun 9–5 🚇 Eastern Market

FOLGER SHAKESPEARE LIBRARY

folger.edu

The world's largest collection of Shakespeare's works is part of this library of 275,000-plus books, manuscripts and paintings from and about the European Renaissance.

🔲 K7 ✉ 201 E Capitol Street SE ☎ 202/544-4600 🕐 Mon–Sat 10–5, Sun 12–5. Garden tours Apr–Oct every 1st and 3rd Sat 🚇 Capitol South 💵 Free; theater performances expensive

FREDERICK DOUGLASS MUSEUM

www3.nahc.org/fd/

The first Washington home of one of the country's most celebrated abolitionists, Douglass lived here for over seven years. It now houses two rooms of memorabilia and the Hall of Fame for Caring Americans.

🔲 K6 ✉ 320 A Street NE ☎ 202/547-4273 🕐 Tours of house by appointment only 🚇 Union Station

GRANT MEMORIAL

Cool and calm Ulysses S. Grant, Civil War general and former president, is honored atop his horse in this memorial, the third largest equestrian statue in the world.

🔲 J6 ✉ 1st Street NW, at foot of Capitol Hill 🕐 Daily 24 hours 🚇 Federal Center SW 💵 Free

NATIONAL POSTAL MUSEUM

postalmuseum.si.edu

Tributes to the Pony Express, 11 million stamps and interactive exhibits illuminate the history of the US Postal Service in this family-oriented museum.

🔲 J5 ✉ 2 Massachusetts Avenue NE across from Union Station ☎ 202/633-5555 🕐 Daily 10–5.30 🚇 Union Station 💵 Free

The Grant Memorial

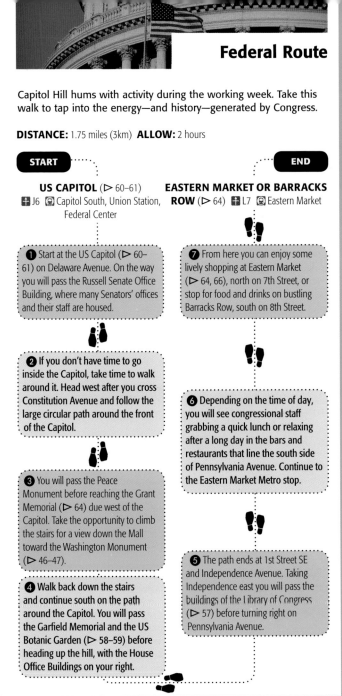

Federal Route

Capitol Hill hums with activity during the working week. Take this walk to tap into the energy—and history—generated by Congress.

DISTANCE: 1.75 miles (3km) **ALLOW:** 2 hours

START

US CAPITOL (▷ 60–61)
🚩 J6 🚇 Capitol South, Union Station, Federal Center

END

EASTERN MARKET OR BARRACKS ROW (▷ 64) 🚩 L7 🚇 Eastern Market

❶ Start at the US Capitol (▷ 60–61) on Delaware Avenue. On the way you will pass the Russell Senate Office Building, where many Senators' offices and their staff are housed.

❷ If you don't have time to go inside the Capitol, take time to walk around it. Head west after you cross Constitution Avenue and follow the large circular path around the front of the Capitol.

❸ You will pass the Peace Monument before reaching the Grant Memorial (▷ 64) due west of the Capitol. Take the opportunity to climb the stairs for a view down the Mall toward the Washington Monument (▷ 46–47).

❹ Walk back down the stairs and continue south on the path around the Capitol. You will pass the Garfield Memorial and the US Botanic Garden (▷ 58–59) before heading up the hill, with the House Office Buildings on your right.

❼ From here you can enjoy some lively shopping at Eastern Market (▷ 64, 66), north on 7th Street, or stop for food and drinks on bustling Barracks Row, south on 8th Street.

❻ Depending on the time of day, you will see congressional staff grabbing a quick lunch or relaxing after a long day in the bars and restaurants that line the south side of Pennsylvania Avenue. Continue to the Eastern Market Metro stop.

❺ The path ends at 1st Street SE and Independence Avenue. Taking Independence east you will pass the buildings of the Library of Congress (▷ 57) before turning right on Pennsylvania Avenue.

CAPITOL HILL WALK

65

Shopping

A. LITTERI

alitteri.com

In the heart of the wholesale market since 1932, this Italian shop stocks more than 100 types of olive oil and wines to go with any pasta dish you can dream up.

➕ L4 ✉ 517 Morse Street NE ☎ 202/544-0183 🕓 Tue–Wed 8–4, Thu 8–5, Fri–Sat 8–6 🚇 New York Avenue, then 10-min walk

CAPITOL HILL BOOKS

capitolhillbooks-dc.com

It's near impossible for this store to stock any more used books. Don't yodel too loud—you might be crushed under an avalanche of books in the bathroom. Seriously.

➕ L7 ✉ 657 C Street SE ☎ 202/544-1621 🕓 Mon–Fri 11.30–6, Sat–Sun 9–6 🚇 Eastern Market

EASTERN MARKET

easternmarket-dc.org

Here you'll find fresh produce under the canopy on weekends and fresh meats, fish, cheeses, baked goods and pre-pared foods six days a week. Saturday also brings a craft market, with a large selection of handmade jewelry.

➕ L7 ✉ 225 7th Street SE 🕓 Tue–Fri 7–7, Sat 7–6, Sun 9–5 🚇 Eastern Market

FAIRY GODMOTHER

This store caters to children of all ages, with a multicultural choice of books and toys.

➕ L7 ✉ 319 7th Street SE ☎ 202/547-5474 🕓 Mon–Fri 10.30–6, Sat 10–5, Sun 10.30–3.30 🚇 Eastern Market

FORECAST

forecaststore.com

Well known for its excellent service and stylish, classic clothing for women, Forecast also stocks gifts, homewares and accessories.

➕ L7 ✉ 218 7th Street SE ☎ 202/547-7337 🕓 Tue–Fri 11–7, Sat 10–6, Sun 12–5 🚇 Eastern Market

GROOVY DC CARDS & GIFTS

groovydc.com

This quirky card and gift shop sells lovely items like journals, photo frames, candles, prints and local art.

➕ L7 ✉ 321 7th Street SE ☎ 202/544-6633 🕓 Mon 12–6, Tue–Fri 11–7, Sat 10–6, Sun 11–5 🚇 Eastern Market

UNION STATION

unionstationdc.com

The city's main transportation hub also doubles as a shopping mall where you can wander along marble-floored avenues. The stores are mostly national and international brands.

➕ K5 ✉ 50 Massachusetts Avenue NE ☎ 202/289-1908 🕓 Mon–Sat 10–9, Sun 12–6 🚇 Union Station

WOVEN HISTORY AND SILK ROAD

wovenhistory.com

Selling Persian and tribal textiles, weavings and rugs, owner Mamet will "charm and disarm" you with his travels and tales, and stories of how he has set up looms in refugee camps.

➕ L7 ✉ 315 7th Street SE ☎ 202/543-1705 🕓 Tue–Sun 10–6 🚇 Eastern Market

MARKET MENU

For fresh produce and artisanal meats, check out Eastern Market (▷ 64 and above), Dupont Circle Market (Q Street NW and Massachusetts Avenue; Jan–Mar Sun 10am–1pm, Mar–Dec Sun 9am–2pm), or Union Market (1309 5th Street NE; daily 8am–8pm).

Entertainment and Nightlife

CAPITOL LOUNGE

capitolloungedc.com

The Cap Lounge is a sports bar at heart and you may be lucky if you're hoping to catch a match on TV.

K7 229 Pennsylvania Avenue SE 202/547-2098 Mon–Wed 4pm–2am, Thu 11am–2am, Fri 11am–3am, Sat–Sun 10.30am–3am Capitol South

COOLIDGE AUDITORIUM

loc.gov

With its near-perfect acoustics and sightlines, this Library of Congress auditorium draws talented musicians from a broad range of genres.

K7 101 Independence Avenue SE 202/707-5502 Capitol South

THE DUBLINER

dublinerdc.com

This Irish pub has been around for more than 40 years, is a favorite with Senate staff, and often features live music.

J5 4 F Street NW 202/737-3773 Sun–Thu 11am–1.30am, Fri–Sat 11am–2.30am Union Station

FOLGER SHAKESPEARE LIBRARY

folger.edu

Daring productions of the Bard's work are staged here in this re-creation of an Elizabethan theater.

K7 201 East Capitol Street SE 202/544-4600 Capitol South

HAWK'N'DOVE

hawkndovedc.com

This dark-wood-panel bar is often frequented by lobbyists and interns.

K7 329 Pennsylvania Avenue SE 202/547-0030 Mon–Thu 11am–2am, Fri 11am–3am, Sat 10am–3am, Sun 10am–2am Capitol South

LOCKHEED MARTIN IMAX THEATER

si.edu/imax

The giant IMAX screen at the National Air and Space Museum (▷ 39) shows larger-than-life nature and space films.

H7 6th Street and Independence Avenue SW 866/868-7444 Check online for times L'Enfant Plaza

SONOMA WINE BAR

sonomadc.com

A soothing bar with exposed brick walls and hardwood floors, Sonoma offers a large selection of wine by the glass and a knowledgeable staff.

K7 223 Pennsylvania Avenue SE 202/544-8088 Dinner daily, lunch Mon–Fri Capitol South

TUNE INN

Enjoy a cold beer in this booth-lined bar overlooked by stuffed animal heads.

K7 331 Pennsylvania Avenue SE 202/542-2725 Mon–Fri 8am–2am, Sat–Sun 8am–3am Capitol South

---

SPECTATOR SPORTS

It's easy to catch a pro-sporting event in DC. The Wizards and Mystics play basketball and the Capitals play hockey at the Verizon Center in Downtown. Baseball fans can head to National Park, where the "Nats" take on the opposition. Buy tickets online or in person at stadium box offices.

MOVIES

Check the daily newspapers for mainstream movies. For art-house and foreign films, try **Landmark's E Street Cinema** (☎ 202/783-9494) or the Angelika Pop-Up at Union Market (550 Penn Street NE). The **Library of Congress** (☎ 202/707-9779) shows classic movies at various locations.

Where to Eat

<table>
<tr><td colspan="2">PRICES</td></tr>
<tr><td colspan="2">Prices are approximate, based on a 3-course meal for one person.</td></tr>
<tr><td>$$$</td><td>over $50</td></tr>
<tr><td>$$</td><td>$30–$50</td></tr>
<tr><td>$</td><td>under $30</td></tr>
</table>

BANANA CAFÉ AND PIANO BAR ($)

bananacafedc.com

Try the Cuban and Puerto Rican dishes at this vibrant eatery with live entertainment each night.

➕ L8 ✉ 500 8th Street SE ☎ 202/543-5906
🕐 Daily lunch, dinner 🚇 Eastern Market

BELGA CAFÉ ($–$$)

belgacafe.com

This smart Belgian restaurant with its subtly flavored options is best at brunch.
➕ L8 ✉ 514 8th Street SE ☎ 202/544-0100
🕐 Daily dinner, Mon–Fri lunch, Sat–Sun brunch
🚇 Eastern Market

FIREHOOK ($)

firehook.com

This popular bakery churns out tasty sandwiches on fresh-baked bread, along with tarts, pies, muffins and pastries.
➕ K7 ✉ 215 Pennsylvania Avenue SE
☎ 202/429-2253 🕐 Mon–Fri 6.30am–7pm,
Sat–Sun 7–5 🚇 Capitol South

GOOD STUFF EATERY ($)

goodstuffeatery.com

Since 2008 chef Spike Mendelsohn has satisfied the nostalgia for American classics like hamburgers and milk shakes. Don't mistake Good Stuff for a run-of-the-mill diner, though: everything is prepared with high-quality ingredients.
➕ K7 ✉ 303 Pennsylvania Avenue SE
☎ 202/543-8222 🕐 Mon–Sat 11am–10pm
🚇 Capitol South

MARKET LUNCH ($)

This counter-service eatery in Eastern Market features crab cakes, fried fish and North Carolina barbecue.
➕ L6 ✉ 225 7th Street SE ☎ 202/547-8444 🕐 Tue–Fri 7.30–2.30, Sat 8–3, Sun 11–3
🚇 Eastern Market

MONTMARTRE ($$)

montmartredc.com

A traditional but exceptional French bistro with an open-plan dining room and friendly environment.
➕ L6 ✉ 327 7th Street SE ☎ 202/544-1244
🕐 Tue–Sun lunch, dinner, Sat–Sun brunch
🚇 Eastern Market

ROSE'S LUXURY ($$–$$$)

rosesluxury.com

Chef Aaron Silverman has been praised for his "Southern comfort food threaded with globe-trotting ingredients." No reservations are accepted.
➕ L8 ✉ 717 8th Street SE ☎ 202/580-8999
🕐 Mon–Sat dinner 🚇 Eastern Market

TED'S BULLETIN ($$)

tedsbulletin.com

The all-day breakfast is one of the draws at this fun, family-friendly establishment, serving up American classics and putting its own twist on milk shakes and even the iconic Pop Tart.
➕ L8 ✉ 505 8th Street SE ☎ 202/544-8337 🕐 Daily breakfast, lunch and dinner
🚇 Eastern Market

UNION MARKET

Just beyond the northern boundary of Capitol Hill, this hub of all things locally made and artisanal offers Rappahannock oysters, tacos, local ice cream, empanadas, craft beer, as well as artisanal meats and fish.

DC's oldest neighborhood started life as a tobacco port. Today well-heeled residents call this huge historic district home, with visitors attracted to Georgetown's outdoor shopping, especially when the sun shines.

Georgetown/Foggy Bottom

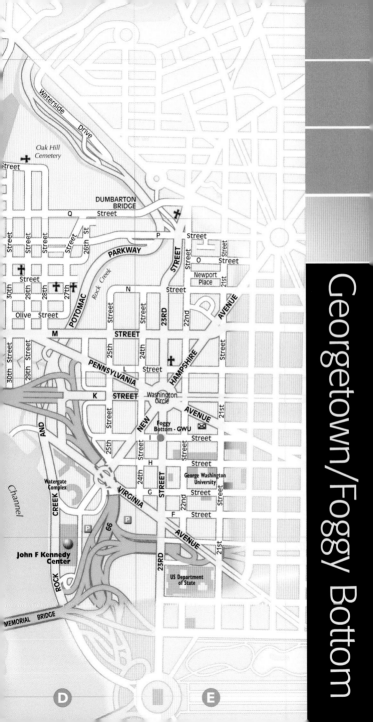

Georgetown at night (left); shopfronts (below); strolling the streets of Georgetown (right)

Georgetown Shopping

The legacy of residents like John and Jackie Kennedy and former *Washington Post* publisher Katharine Graham continues to give Georgetown an exclusive air, even though the village's heyday as the center of Washington's political and social life has passed. So it's no wonder that top-of-the-line retailers consider a Georgetown storefront highly desirable, with charming Federal-era buildings adding to the appeal.

Wisconsin and M Metro inaccessibility does not deter crowds from Georgetown's main intersection, full of chic shops that stretch north on Wisconsin Avenue and east on M Street. Warm months are particularly busy as tourists and locals flock to the shops they know, such as Banana Republic, Urban Outfitters and Coach, as well as high-end beauty brands, among countless others.

Not just an outdoor mall You'll also find boutiques, antiques shops, home furnishings and bookstores. Dubbed "Georgetown's Design District," Cady's Alley, off 33rd Street just south of M Street, is lined with mid- to high-end home furnishing galleries. Georgetown's fine antiques shops can be found mainly on the eastern section of M Street before it crosses Rock Creek Parkway. Some of the better independent shops huddle farther up Wisconsin Avenue on Book Hill, just south of the Georgetown Library.

THE BASICS

+ C4

✉ Mainly M Street NW between 30th Street and 34th Street and Wisconsin Avenue NW between South Street and R Street

♿ Limited

HIGHLIGHTS

● The shops at Georgetown
● A stroll along the C&O Canal towpath
● The view from the Georgetown Library
● Wandering among the Federalist mansions to the northeast of the intersection between Wisconsin Avenue and M Street

John F. Kennedy Center

TOP 25

A bust of Kennedy inside the Kennedy Center

THE BASICS

kennedy-center.org

🚩 D6

✉ 2700 F Street NW

☎ 202/416-8340; 800/444-1324

🕐 Tours every 10 min Mon–Fri 10–5, Sat–Sun 10–1

💵 Free tours; performance ticket prices vary

♿ Excellent

🍽 KC Café, Roof Terrace Restaurant ☎ 202/416-8555 for reservations

🕐 Café daily 11.30–8; restaurant dinner 5–8 before performances; brunch 11–2 most Sun

🚇 Foggy Bottom. Free shuttle bus every 15 min Mon–Fri 9.45am to midnight, Sat 10am–midnight, Sun 12–12, federal holidays 4–midnight

❓ Tours Mon–Fri 10–5, Sat–Sun 10–1. Free Millennium Stage performance daily at 6pm

HIGHLIGHTS

● Hall of States
● View from the roof terrace
● Henri Matisse tapestries
● Well-stocked gift shop

With seven theaters, this national cultural center covers 8 acres (3ha) and is the jewel of the city's arts scene. The roof terrace provides a stunning 360-degree view of Washington and the Potomac.

The seat of the arts Opened in 1971, Edward Durell Stone's white-marble box overlooks the Potomac River next to the Watergate complex. The Center's inaugural performance featured the world premiere of a Requiem mass honoring President Kennedy, a work commissioned from composer and conductor Leonard Bernstein. As a living memorial to President Kennedy, the Center now hosts more than 3,000 performances a year by some of the world's most talented artists.

The interior The red carpet in the Hall of States, and the parallel Hall of Nations, leads to the Grand Foyer, where visitors are greeted by a 3,000lb (1,363kg) bronze bust of President Kennedy. The 630ft (192m) long hall blazes from the light of 16 Orrefors crystal chandeliers, donated by Sweden and reflected in 58ft-high (17.5m) mirrors, a gift from Belgium. If you go on the tour, you'll see many other works of art and gifts from more than 60 countries. One end of the hall is devoted to the Millennium Stage, where free performances are given every evening. The building also contains an opera house, a concert hall, two stage theaters, a jazz club and a theater lab, and there's a major expansion project underway.

More to See

CHESAPEAKE & OHIO CANAL

nps.gov/choh

This tree-lined canal runs along-side the Potomac River from Georgetown (the path begins behind the Four Seasons Hotel) to Maryland. Mule-drawn canal boats are operated by the National Park Service from the Great Falls visitor center in Potomac, MD.

➕ C4 ✉ C&O Canal Visitor Center: 1057 Thomas Jefferson Street NW ☎ Canal boat rides 301/767-3714 (Sat, Sun 11, 1.30, 3) ⊕ Visitor Center: Wed–Sun 9–4.30 (summer only) 🚇 Foggy Bottom, then 15-min walk 💲 Free. Canal boat tour moderate; under 3 free

DUMBARTON OAKS

doaks.org

In 1944, the conference leading to the formation of the United Nations was held at this estate, also known for its formal garden, with an orangery, rose garden, wisteria and shaded terraces. This is a must-visit for anyone interested in gardens.

➕ C3 ✉ 31st and R streets NW ☎ 202/339-6401 ⊕ Museum Tue–Sun 11.30–5.30; garden 2–6 (closes 5pm Nov–14 Mar) 🚇 Dupont Circle, then bus D2 or DC Circulator bus 💲 Garden moderate; museum free

KREEGER MUSEUM

kreegermuseum.org

Built by David and Carmen Kreeger, this Philip Johnson mansion now houses art, mainly the work of male masters of the last two centuries.

➕ Off map at A3 ✉ 2401 Foxhall Road NW ☎ 202/338-3552 ⊕ Tue–Thu tours 10.30, 1.30 (reservations required), Fri–Sat 10–4 (no reservations required) 🚇 Tenleytown, then taxi 💲 Expensive

THE OLD STONE HOUSE

nps.gov/olst

The oldest house in the city, dating from 1765, commemorates the daily lives of the early residents of Georgetown.

➕ D4 ✉ 3051 M Street NW ☎ 202/426-6851 ⊕ Daily 11–6 🚇 Foggy Bottom, then 10-min walk 💲 Free

Towpath of the Chesapeake & Ohio Canal

The oldest house in Washington, the Old Stone House

Waterfront Walk

See one of Washington's oldest and most stately neighborhoods from a variety of angles and perspectives.

DISTANCE: 1.5 miles (2.5km) **ALLOW:** 2 hours

START

JOHN F. KENNEDY CENTER
(▷ 74) 🚻 D6 🚇 Foggy Bottom

END

GEORGETOWN UNIVERSITY
🚻 B4 🚇 Rosslyn (a 20-min walk)

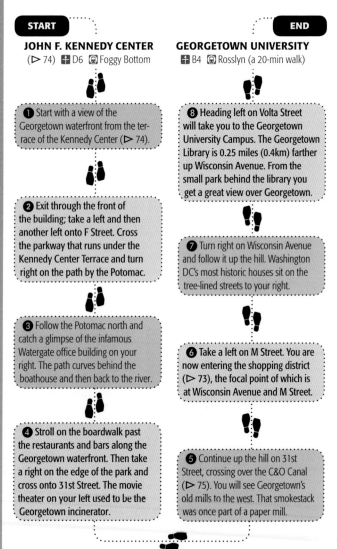

❶ Start with a view of the Georgetown waterfront from the terrace of the Kennedy Center (▷ 74).

❷ Exit through the front of the building; take a left and then another left onto F Street. Cross the parkway that runs under the Kennedy Center Terrace and turn right on the path by the Potomac.

❸ Follow the Potomac north and catch a glimpse of the infamous Watergate office building on your right. The path curves behind the boathouse and then back to the river.

❹ Stroll on the boardwalk past the restaurants and bars along the Georgetown waterfront. Then take a right on the edge of the park and cross onto 31st Street. The movie theater on your left used to be the Georgetown incinerator.

❽ Heading left on Volta Street will take you to the Georgetown University Campus. The Georgetown Library is 0.25 miles (0.4km) farther up Wisconsin Avenue. From the small park behind the library you get a great view over Georgetown.

❼ Turn right on Wisconsin Avenue and follow it up the hill. Washington DC's most historic houses sit on the tree-lined streets to your right.

❻ Take a left on M Street. You are now entering the shopping district (▷ 73), the focal point of which is at Wisconsin Avenue and M Street.

❺ Continue up the hill on 31st Street, crossing over the C&O Canal (▷ 75). You will see Georgetown's old mills to the west. That smokestack was once part of a paper mill.

Shopping

2ND TIME AROUND

2ndtimearound.com

This high-end consignment shop sells designer clothes and accessories in great condition.

🔳 C4 ✉ 3289 M Street NW ☎ 202/333-2355 🕐 Mon–Sat 10–7, Sun 12–6 🚇 Foggy Bottom, then 15-min walk

A MANO

amano.bz

A Mano (By Hand) stocks fine home furnishings crafted by European artisans.

🔳 C3 ✉ 1677 Wisconsin Avenue NW ☎ 202/298-7200 🕐 Mon–Sat 10–6, Sun 12–5 🚇 Foggy Bottom, then 15-min walk

ANTHROPOLOGIE

anthropologie.com

A magnet of shabby chic carrying homeware, clothing and accessories.

🔳 C4 ✉ 3222 M Street NW ☎ 202/337-1363 🕐 Mon–Sat 10–9, Sun 12–7 🚇 Foggy Bottom, then 15-min walk

BRIDGE STREET BOOKS

bridgestreetbooks.com

This charming row house contains a good collection of books.

🔳 D4 ✉ 2814 Pennsylvania Avenue NW ☎ 202/965-5200 🕐 Mon–Thu 11–9, Fri–Sat 11–10, Sun 12–6 🚇 Foggy Bottom, then 10-min walk

SECRET ALLEY

Down a cobblestone side street is Georgetown's design district, Cady's Alley, with its high-end home furnishing and fashion designers complementing the local antiques stores. The historic shops open up onto a quaint courtyard where Leopold's Kafe and Konditorei (▷ 80) offers delicious Austrian-inspired gastronomic delights.

DEAN AND DELUCA

deandeluca.com

A picnicker's paradise, this grocer carries the finest fruit, chocolate and cheese and a dazzling array of gourmet foods.

🔳 C4 ✉ 3276 M Street NW ☎ 202/342-2500 🕐 Mon–Sat 8am–9pm, Sun 8–8 🚇 Foggy Bottom, then 15-min walk

DESIGN WITHIN REACH

dwr.com

Modern home furnishings from well-known designers from around the world set in gallery displays.

🔳 C4 ✉ 3307 Cady's Alley, 3306 M Street NW ☎ 202/339-9480 🕐 Mon–Sat 10–6, Sun 12–6 🚇 Foggy Bottom, then 15-min walk

HU'S SHOES

husonline.com

On the absolute front edge of fashion, Hu's carries shoes you can't find outside of New York, Paris or Milan.

🔳 D4 ✉ 3005 M Street NW (also 2906 M Street) ☎ 202/342-0202 🕐 Mon–Sat 10–7, Sun 12–5 🚇 Foggy Bottom, then 15-min walk

INTERMIX

intermixonline.com

Intermix offers hand-picked styles from the "it" list of designers, including the UK's popular Stella McCartney.

🔳 C4 ✉ 3300 M Street NW ☎ 202/298-8080 🕐 Mon–Wed 11–7, Thu–Sat 11–8, Sun 12–6 🚇 Foggy Bottom, then 15-min walk

JEAN PIERRE ANTIQUES

jeanpierreantiques.com

There's no need to go to France: Enjoy this Georgetown shop that supplies antique furniture to well-heeled locals and famous visitors.

🔳 D4 ✉ 2601 P Street NW ☎ 202/337-1731 🕐 Mon–Fri 11–5, Sat–Sun 12–5 🚇 Dupont Circle, then 15-min walk

JUST PAPER AND TEA

justpaperandtea.com

Just Paper and Tea sells just that. It's home to a large selection of fine paper and quality stationery and a wide range of loose and bagged artisan teas.

🔲 C4 ✉ 3232 P Street NW ☎ 202/333-9141 🕐 Tue–Sat 10–5 (by appointment only on Sun 12–4) 🚌 DC Circulator bus

KIEHL'S

kiehls.com

Kiehl's has had a strong following for its skincare products since opening as an apothecary in 1851.

🔲 D4 ✉ 3110 M Street NW ☎ 202/333-5101 🕐 Mon–Sat 10–7, Sun 12–6 🚇 Foggy Bottom, then 10-min walk

THE OLD PRINT GALLERY

oldprintgallery.com

This gallery stocks antique prints as old as America itself, as well as an impressive collection of *New Yorker* covers.

🔲 C4 ✉ 1220 31st Street NW ☎ 202/965-1818 🕐 Tue–Sat 10–5.20 🚇 Foggy Bottom, then 15-min walk

PAPER SOURCE

paper-source.com

This two-floor paper store stocks cards, fine stationery and craft kits. Many of their products feature designs from Paper Source's own design team.

🔲 D4 ✉ 3019 M Street NW ☎ 202/298-5545 🕐 Mon–Sat 10–9, Sun 11–7 🚇 Foggy Bottom, then 10-min walk

Entertainment and Nightlife

BIRRERIA PARADISO

eatyourpizza.com

Downstairs from Pizzeria Paradiso (▷ 80), this temple of beer has 16 of the world's finest varieties on tap and 80 in bottles.

🔲 C4 ✉ 3282 M Street NW ☎ 202/337-1245 🕐 Mon–Thu 11.30–10, Fri–Sat 11.30–11, Sun 12–10 🚇 Foggy Bottom

BLUES ALLEY

bluesalley.com

A legendary jazz club, Blues Alley was founded in 1965 and made famous by the likes of Dizzy Gillespie and Charlie Byrd. It's now a venue that pulls in top national acts.

🔲 C4 ✉ Rear of 1073 Wisconsin Avenue NW ☎ 202/337-4141 🕐 Daily 6pm–12.30am 🚇 Foggy Bottom, then 15-min walk

CLYDE'S

clydes.com/georgetown

Clyde's is a great saloon to call into for a drink. It's decked out in dark-wood paneling and has a solid oak bar. There's also a solid menu to choose from.

🔲 C4 ✉ 3236 M Street NW ☎ 202/333-9180 🕐 Mon–Thu 11am–midnight, Fri 11am–1am, Sat 10am–1am, Sun 9am–midnight 🚇 Foggy Bottom, then 15-min walk

HALF-PRICE TICKETS

TICKETplace (ticketplace.org) offers same-day half-price tickets (available online only) to a variety of shows around town. There is a variable service charge, so be sure to check what you are paying. Many theaters also sell discounted preview week or last-minute tickets.

DEGREES

ritzcarlton.com

This elegant watering hole in the lobby of the Ritz-Carlton draws well-dressed patrons. You'll be served great cocktails while sitting at the sleek black slate bar.
➕ C4 ✉ Ritz-Carlton Hotel, 3100 South Street NW ☎ 202/912-4100 🕐 Daily breakfast, lunch, dinner 🚇 Foggy Bottom, then 15-min walk

GYPSY SALLY'S

gypsysallys.com

A comfortable and friendly music venue with food and drinks on offer, all tucked under the Whitehurst Freeway.
➕ C4 ✉ 3401 K Street NW ☎ 202/333-7700 🕐 Tue–Sat 5.30 til late 🚇 Foggy Bottom, then 10-min walk

J PAUL'S

jpaulsdc.com

A popular bar in an historic building. Students and tourists rub shoulders with politicians and journalists.
➕ C4 ✉ 3218 M Street NW ☎ 202/333-3450 🕐 Mon–Thu 11.30am–2am, Fri 11.30am–3am, Sat 10.30am–3am, Sun 10.30am–2am 🚇 Foggy Bottom, then 15-min walk

JOHN F. KENNEDY CENTER

DC's top spot for renowned performers (▷ 74).

MARTIN'S TAVERN

martinstavern.com

This distinguished but unpretentious saloon was a favorite of a young JFK and Jackie. Dark leather booths are named after the famous presidential faces who have dined here.
➕ C4 ✉ 1264 Wisconsin Avenue NW ☎ 202/333-7370 🕐 Mon–Thu 11am–1.30am, Fri 11am–2.30am, Sat 9am–2.30am, Sun 8am–1.30am 🚇 Foggy Bottom, then 15-min walk

MATÉ

matedc.com

Kitted out in red, Maté offers sushi and ceviche, as well as specialty cocktails. There's live music on the weekend.
➕ C5 ✉ 3101 K Street NW ☎ 202/333-2006 🕐 Sun–Thu 4pm–12.30am, Fri–Sat 5pm–1am 🚇 Foggy Bottom, then 15-min walk

SEQUOIA

arkrestaurants.com/sequoia

On the waterfront with a lovely view over the river, the bar at Sequoia is a popular place for a drink.
➕ D5 ✉ 3000 K Street NW ☎ 202/944-4200 🕐 Daily lunch, dinner 🚇 Foggy Bottom, then 15-min walk

THOMPSON BOAT CENTER

thompsonboatcenter.com

See the city from the water and rent a canoe, rowing shell or kayak.
➕ D5 ✉ 2900 Virginia Avenue NW ☎ 202/333-9543 🕐 Rentals mid-Mar to Oct daily 8–5 🚇 Foggy Bottom, then 15-min walk

THE TOMBS

tombs.com

This subterranean bar, adorned with vintage crew prints and oars, is popular among students.
➕ B4 ✉ 1226 36th Street NW ☎ 202/337-6668 🕐 Mon–Thu 11.30am–1.30am, Fri–Sat 11.30am–2.30am, Sun 9.30am–1.30am 🚇 Foggy Bottom, then 15-min walk

BARBECUE BATTLE

One weekend every June barbecuers from around the country gather on Pennsylvania Avenue NW between 9th and 14th streets to face off. But it's not just about the flames. Entertainment includes live rock, jazz and blues acts and cooking demonstrations. Tickets are available at bbqindc.com.

Where to Eat

PRICES
Prices are approximate, based on a 3-course meal for one person.
$$$ over $50
$$ $30–$50
$ under $30

1789 ($$$)

1789restaurant.com

In a town house with a large fireplace, 1789 specializes in innovatively prepared game and seafood.

🚩 B4 ✉ 1226 36th Street NW ☎ 202/965-1789 🕐 Mon–Thu 6–10, Fri 6–11, Sat 5.30–11, Sun 5.30–10 🚇 Foggy Bottom, then bus 32 or 38B

BISTRO FRANÇAIS ($$$)

bistrofrancaisdc.com

Delicious classic French cuisine is served at this award-winning restaurant. With crisp, white tablecloths and vintage French posters, you could be in Paris.

🚩 C4 ✉ 3124 M Street NW ☎ 202/338-3830 🕐 Sun–Thu 11am–3am, Fri–Sat 11am–4am 🚇 Foggy Bottom, then 15-min walk

BOURBON STEAK ($$$)

bourbonsteakdc.com

Dry-aged beef poached in butter prior to grilling is the star at this steakhouse in the Four Seasons Hotel. Great fish dishes, a range of cocktails and attentive service are more reasons why Bourbon Steak is considered the city's best.

🚩 C4 ✉ 2800 Pennsylvania Avenue NW ☎ 202/393-2900 🕐 Mon–Fri 11.30am–2.30pm, Sun–Thu 6–10pm, Fri–Sat 6–10.30pm 🚇 Foggy Bottom

CHEZ BILLY SUD ($$$)

chezbillysud.com

The draws at this charming intimate bistro are the handcrafted cocktails and expertly prepared dishes inspired by the cuisine of Southern France.

🚩 C4 ✉ 1039 31st Street NW ☎ 202/965-2606 🕐 Daily dinner, lunch Tue–Sun, weekend brunch 🚇 Foggy Bottom, then 15-min walk

FIOLA MARE ($$$)

fiolamaredc.com

"The city's most sumptuous spot for seafood," says The Washington Post. That and handmade pastas have made this one of DC's in-demand dining rooms.

🚩 D5 ✉ 3050 K Street NW ☎ 202/628-0065 🕐 Tue–Fri lunch, daily dinner, weekend brunch 🚇 Foggy Bottom, then 15-min walk

LEOPOLD'S KAFE AND KONDITOREI ($$$)

kafeleopolds.com

This Austrian café offers dishes ranging from schnitzel to a delicious selection of salads. Leopold's also has a huge pastry selection. Everything is served à la carte.

🚩 C4 ✉ 3315 M Street NW ☎ 202/965-6005 🕐 Daily breakfast, lunch, dinner 🚇 Foggy Bottom, then 15-min walk

MISS SAIGON ($–$$)

ms-saigonus.com

An extensive menu of traditional Vietnamese dishes is expertly prepared at this popular, atmospheric restaurant.

🚩 D4 ✉ 3057 M Street NW ☎ 202/333-5545 🕐 Sun–Thu 11.30–10.30, Fri–Sat 11.30–11 🚇 Foggy Bottom, then 15-min walk

PIZZERIA PARADISO ($)

eatyourpizza.com

The stone, wood-burning oven is the heart of this restaurant, which pumps out the best Neapolitan pizza in town.

🚩 C4 ✉ 3282 M Street NW ☎ 202/337-1245 🕐 Mon–Tue 11.30–10, Wed–Thu 11.30–11, Fri–Sat 11.30am–midnight, Sun 12–10 🚇 Foggy Bottom, then 15-min walk

Mostly residential, Northwest Washington is home to shady streets, embassies and the expansive Rock Creek Park. With more than its fair share of bars and restaurants, it's also a popular nighttime destination.

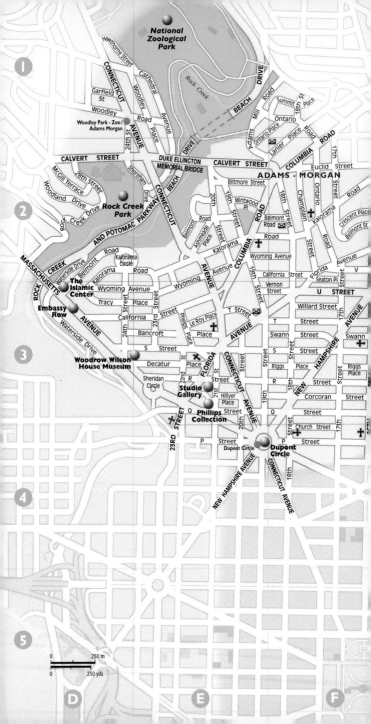

National
Zoological
Park

Rock Creek

BEACH
DRIVE

Summit
Place
18th
Ontario

Adams Mill Road
Ontario Place
Lanier Place
COLUMBIA ROAD
17th Street
Euclid Street

Hawthorne Street

CONNECTICUT AVENUE
Woodley Road
Cathedral Avenue
Woodley Place
Garfield St
Woodley
24th Street

Woodley Park - Zoo / Adams Morgan

1

CALVERT STREET
DUKE ELLINGTON
MEMORIAL BRIDGE
CALVERT STREET

ADAMS - MORGAN

McGill Terrace
28th Street
Woodland Drive

Shoreham Drive

BEACH DRIVE

CONNECTICUT AVENUE

Biltmore Street
Mintwood Pl

Champlain Street
Ontario Road
Kalorama Road
Crescent Place
Belmont St

2

Rock Creek Park

ROCK CREEK
AND POTOMAC PARKWAY

Belmont Road
Ashmeade Place
20th Street
19th Street
Kalorama Road

Belmont Road

Wyoming Avenue
California Street
Vernon Street
Florida Avenue
Seaton Pl
V

MASSACHUSETTS

Waterside Drive
Belmont Road
Kalorama Road
Kalorama Circle
Road
Kalorama

ROCK CREEK

The Islamic Center

Wyoming Avenue
Tracy Place
24th Street
23rd Street

CONNECTICUT AVENUE
COLUMBIA ROAD

U STREET

NEW HAMPSHIRE AVENUE
17th Street

Willard Street
Street
Swann Street
Swann Street

Embassy Row

AVENUE

California Street
Bancroft Place
Phelps Place
Le Roy Place
T Street

T Street
S Street
Riggs Place
Riggs Place

3

Waterside Drive

S Street
Decatur Place
Sheridan Circle
2nd Street
FLORIDA
3rd Street
R Street
Hillyer Place

New Hampshire

19th Street
18th Street

Woodrow Wilson House Museum

Studio Gallery

Phillips Collection

Q Street
P Street
Corcoran Street
R Street
Church Street

23RD STREET
20th Street

P Street
Dupont Circle

Dupont Circle

CONNECTICUT AVENUE
18th Street

4

NEW HAMPSHIRE AVENUE

5

0   250 m
0   250 yds

D   **E**   **F**

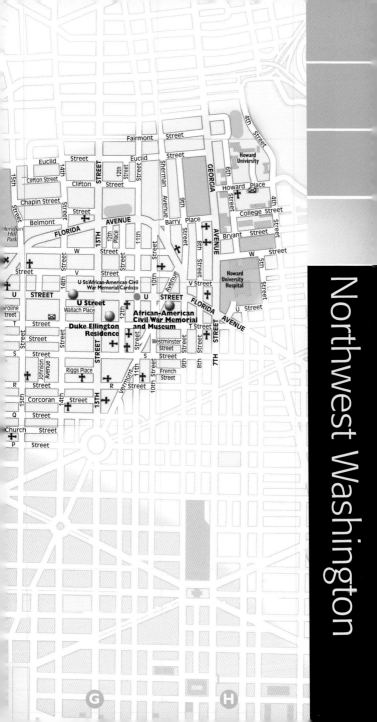

Fairmont Street

Euclid Street
Clifton Street
Chapin Street
Belmont Street
FLORIDA AVENUE
Euclid Street
Clifton Street

15th Street
14th Street
Meridian Hill Park

13TH STREET
12th Place

Howard University

GEORGIA AVENUE
6th Street
Howard Place
College Street
Bryant Street

9th Street

Sherman Avenue

Barry Place

8th Street

W Street
V Street

4th Street

5th Street

Howard University Hospital

W Street
U Street

FLORIDA AVENUE

U STREET
Caroline Street
U Street
Wallach Place

14th Street

U St/African-American Civil War Memorial/Cardozo
U Street

U STREET
Duke Ellington Residence

11th Street
10th Street
Vermont Avenue

African-American Civil War Memorial and Museum

Westminster Street
S Street
French Street

9th Street
8th Street

7TH STREET

T Street

T Street
Street
Street
S Street

Johnson Avenue
Riggs Place

R Street

15th Street
14th Street

13TH STREET

Corcoran Street

Q Street
Church Street
P Street

G

H

Northwest Washington

National Zoological Park

TOP 25

A panda (left) and a male lion (right) at the National Zoological Park

THE BASICS

nationalzoo.si.edu

➕ E1

✉ 3001 Connecticut Avenue NW

☎ 202/633-4888

🕐 Grounds: Apr–Oct daily 6am–8pm; Nov–Mar 6–6. Animal buildings: Apr–Oct daily 10–6; Nov–Mar 10–4.30

🎫 Free. Parking charge

♿ Excellent

🍴 Snack bars, cafés

Ⓜ Woodley Park–Zoo

HIGHLIGHTS

- Bei Bei, the panda cub
- Amazonia
- Orangutans on the "O line"
- Bird House
- Elephants
- Lions, tigers and cheetahs
- Kids' Farm
- Weekend walking tours

Founded in 1889, this 163-acre (66ha) park, one of America's finest zoos, is home to more than 2,000 animals from over 400 species. Come here to see seals swim, monkeys swing and meerkats dart.

Before elephants and donkeys A national zoo was the vision of William Hornaday, who was a taxidermist at the Smithsonian. Hornaday opened a trial zoo, packed with animals including bears and bison, right outside the Smithsonian Castle on the Mall. Not surprisingly, Congress soon approved a site a little farther away in Rock Creek Park, which the zoo still calls home. Plans for the spot were drawn up by Hornaday and Frederick Law Olmsted, Jr., son of the designer of Central Park in New York. When Hornaday was not chosen as the first director of the zoo, he left and founded the Bronx Zoo.

America's park More than two million people a year visit the zoo. Its most popular inhabitant is the male panda cub Bei Bei, who was born in August 2015. Bao Bao, his sister, also lives at the zoo. Their parents Mei Xiang and Tian Tian replaced the famous Ling-Ling and Hsing-Hsing that were gifts from China following President Nixon's historic visit in 1972. Visitors also come to see the big cats, the "O line," which allows orangutans to swing freely, Amazonia and the Reptile Discovery Center. The bison were reintroduced to celebrate the zoo's 125th anniversary in 2014.

The former home of Duncan Phillips, housing the Phillips Collection, a gallery of modern art

Phillips Collection

This collection in the former house of Duncan Phillips was America's first museum of modern art. It is world-renowned for its collection of Impressionist and Postimpressionist paintings.

Duncan Phillips After the premature death of his father and brother, Phillips established a gallery in their honor in a room of his Georgian Revival home, and it was opened to the public in 1921. Over the years, Phillips and his wife Marjorie, a painter, continued to buy art with a keen eye. Phillips believed strongly in an art lineage—that artists were clearly influenced by their predecessors as they were in turn by those who came before them. The size of his collection grew to more than 3,000 works, including some selections that were risky at the time—Georgia O'Keeffe, Mark Rothko and Pierre Bonnard. They also bought Auguste Renior's *Luncheon of the Boating Party* for a record price of $125,000. In 1930, Phillips moved out and the collection took over. He continued to direct the gallery until his death in 1966.

Current works The permanent collection contains works by Piet Mondrian, Paul Klee, Pablo Picasso, Monet, Degas, Matisse, van Gogh, Cézanne and many well-known American artists. It holds one of the largest collections of works by Arthur Dove (1880–1946), regarded as the first American abstract painter.

THE BASICS

phillipscollection.org

✚ E3

✉ 1600 21st Street NW

☎ 202/387-2151

🕐 Tue–Sat 10–5 (Thu until 8.30), Sun 12–7. Closed public hols

✋ Permanent collection: free weekdays, expensive Sat–Sun. Expensive for temporary exhibitions

♿ Excellent

🍴 Café

Ⓜ Dupont Circle

❓ Tue–Fri short tours noon, 15-min talk on different works of art. Concerts in the Music Room Sep–May Sun 4pm

HIGHLIGHTS

● *Luncheon of the Boating Party*, Auguste Renoir
● *The Rothko Room*, Mark Rothko
● *Repentant St. Peter*, El Greco
● *Entrance to the Public Garden at Arles*, Vincent van Gogh
● *Dancers at the Barre*, Edgar Degas
● *The Migration Series*, Jacob Lawrence

Rock Creek Park

Rock Creek Park in fall (left); Rock Creek (right)

THE BASICS

nps.gov/rocr

🔲 D2

✉ Nature Center, 5200 Glover Road NW

☎ 202/895-6000; Nature Center 202/895-6070

🕐 Nature Center: Wed–Sun 9–5. Grounds: daylight hours

💵 Free

🚇 Friendship Heights then E-2 or E-3 bus

HIGHLIGHTS

- Rock Creek Parkway
- Running and biking trails
- Carter Barron Amphitheater
- Nature Center and Planetarium
- Peirce Mill
- Extensive hiking trails

A geological rift that slices through northwest DC, Rock Creek Park is one of the few metropolitan parks to be shaped mainly by its geology, not the work of man. It's a popular park among the city's residents.

Park of presidents In 1890, President Benjamin Harrison (1833–1901) signed a bill establishing Rock Creek Park as one of the first national parks. The area, over 1,700 acres (687ha), was acquired for a little more than $1 million. While in office, President Theodore Roosevelt, an avid naturalist, would often spend his afternoons hiking in unmarked sections of the park with the French Ambassador, making sure to return after dark so that his appearance "would scandalize no one." Rock Creek Parkway, on the National Registry of Historic Places, was built from 1923 to 1936. During his presidency, Woodrow Wilson would have his driver drop him off in the park with the woman he was courting and then pick them up farther down the road.

Playground of Washingtonians At twice the size of Central Park, Rock Creek Park has enough room for everyone. A paved bike trail leads from the Lincoln Memorial all the way to Maryland, and Beach Drive north of Military Road is closed to motor traffic on the weekends during the day. The park is full of hiking trails and picnic areas, as well as a golf course, tennis courts and horse center.

Washington National Cathedral

The Cathedral, seen from the Bishop's Garden (left); interior of cathedral (right)

The soaring Gothic cathedral is often the setting for national commemorations in times of celebration, crisis and sorrow. Its official name is the Cathedral Church of Saint Peter and Saint Paul in the City and Diocese of Washington, but everyone knows it as the National Cathedral.

Presidential past Three US presidents have had their state funeral here: Dwight Eisenhower, Ronald Reagan and Gerald Ford. Several others were honored with prayer or memorial services after their deaths, including John F. Kennedy, Franklin D. Roosevelt, Calvin Coolidge and Harry S. Truman. Fittingly, a number of presidential inauguration prayer services have been held here, including one for Barack Obama in 2009.

Solid foundation The first foundation stone—made of Indiana limestone—was laid in 1907, and the last wasn't set in place until 83 years later, in 1990. Four architects and thousands of masons and sculptors, among other workers, labored to create the majestic Gothic structure, whose tallest tower reaches 300ft (90m) into the sky. In 2011, the cathedral sustained major damage when a 5.8 magnitude earthquake shook the city and the surrounding area. Stones on several pinnacles broke off, gargoyles and other carvings were damaged, and falling stone punched a hole in the roof. The cathedral was closed for several months after the earthquake and repairs, which were still going on in 2016, have been estimated at $26 million.

THE BASICS

cathedral.org

⊞ B1

✉ 3101 Wisconsin Avenue NW

☎ 202/537-6200

🕐 Mon–Fri 10–5.30, Sat 10–4.30 (Sun services)

💰 Expensive

Ⓜ Dupont Circle, then N2, N3, N4 or N6 bus

❓ Tours 10–11.15, 1–3.30; Mon and Wed 12.30 organ demonstrations

HIGHLIGHTS

● Exterior gargoyles
● Bell tower with two sets of bells (53-bell carillon and 10-bell peal)
● Pulpit carved from stones from Canterbury Cathedral
● The Great Organ, installed in 1938
● Pilgrim Observation Gallery
● Sculpture of Darth Vader on top of northwest tower (binoculars required)

More to See

AFRICAN-AMERICAN CIVIL WAR MEMORIAL AND MUSEUM

afroamcivilwar.org

This museum tells the story of the 209,145 African-Americans who fought to abolish slavery in the American Civil War. Edward Hamilton's bronze memorial, across the street from the museum, was dedicated in 1998.

➕ H3 ✉ 1925 Vermont Avenue NW ☎ 202/667-2667 ⏱ Museum Tue–Fri 10–6.30, Sat 10–4, Sun 12–4; Memorial daily 24 hours 🚇 U Street/African-American Civil War Memorial/Cardozo 🎟 Free

BISHOP'S GARDEN

Winding paths, perennial borders and rustic stone walls make this Washington National Cathedral garden an oasis from urban bustle.

➕ B1 ✉ Wisconsin and Massachusetts Avenues NW ☎ 202/537-2937 ⏱ Daily dawn–dusk 🚇 Dupont Circle, then N2, N3, N4 or N6 bus 🎟 Free

DUPONT CIRCLE

DC's original cosmopolitan enclave, Dupont remains a dynamic pedestrian-friendly neighborhood, site of the city's only year-round farmers' market. In warmer months, the grassy areas team with people.

➕ E4 🚇 Dupont Circle

EDWARD KENNEDY "DUKE" ELLINGTON RESIDENCE

Though born at 1217 22nd Street NW, "Duke" Ellington (1899–1974) grew up on this street and took piano lessons nearby.

➕ G3 ✉ 1805–1816 13th Street NW ⏱ Not open to public 🚇 U Street/African-American Civil War Memorial/Cardozo

EMBASSY ROW

Many of the capital's most beautiful embassies line Massachusetts Avenue north of Dupont Circle.

➕ D3 🚇 Dupont Circle

THE ISLAMIC CENTER

theislamiccenter.com

Calls to the faithful emanate from the 162ft (49m) minaret of this mosque, built in 1957. The inside is adorned with Persian carpets, carvings, stained glass and mosaics.

➕ D3 ✉ 2551 Massachusetts Avenue NW ☎ 202/332-8343 ⏱ Cultural Center: daily 10–5; mosque: between prayer times 🚇 Dupont Circle

STUDIO GALLERY

studiogallerydc.com

Artists in the DC area contribute to the ever-changing exhibitions of contemporary art showcased here.

➕ E3 ✉ 2108 R Street NW ☎ 202/232-8734 ⏱ Wed–Fri 1–6, Sat 11–6 🚇 Dupont Circle

U STREET

U Street was a mecca for jazz musicians and a hub of DC's black community. Live music, bars and gleaming apartments now lure new residents to city life.

➕ G3 ✉ U Street between 10th and 15th streets 🚇 U Street/African-American Civil War Memorial/Cardozo

WOODROW WILSON HOUSE MUSEUM

woodrowwilsonhouse.org

Woodrow Wilson lived here from 1921 until his death in 1924.

➕ D3 ✉ 2340 S Street ☎ 202/387-4062 ⏱ Wed–Sun 10–4 🚇 Dupont Circle 🎟 Expensive

Cosmopolitan Washington

Dupont's tree-lined streets and Circle offer a glimpse of both young DC and elegant, old-fashioned architecture.

DISTANCE: 2.5 miles (4km) **ALLOW:** 1 hour 30 minutes

START

DUPONT CIRCLE (▷ 88)
🕂 E4 🚇 Dupont Circle

END

DUPONT CIRCLE (▷ 88)
🕂 E4 🚇 Dupont Circle

❶ Begin at Dupont Circle Metro's Q Street exit. Go east on Q past Thomas F. Schneider's town houses (1889–92) and the Cairo Apartments (1894).

❷ Turn right on 17th Street, a bustling strip in sunny weather. Take another right on Church Street, which passes some lovely Dupont town houses. Turn left on 18th Street and then right on P Street.

❸ Before you cross over into the Circle, look right to check out the Patterson House, where President Coolidge lived while the White House was being renovated. Many photos of Charles Lindbergh show him waving from this balcony.

❹ Pass into the Circle with the Dupont Memorial Fountain, designed by Lincoln Memorial sculptor Daniel French. Head southwest (roughly left) on New Hampshire Avenue to 1307, the "Brewmaster's Castle."

❽ Turn left onto Decatur Place, left onto Florida Avenue and continue to Connecticut Avenue; Dupont Circle Metro is down the hill.

❼ Past Sheridan Circle, turn right on S Street, which runs along a hilltop park. Walk down the Decatur stairs on your right.

❻ On Massachusetts you will pass the Phillips Collection (▷ 85) and the Anderson House, home of the Society of the Cincinnati.

❺ Turn right onto 20th, then left onto Massachusetts. On the left is the Walsh Mansion, purchased in 1951 by Indonesia for a tenth of the $3 million it cost to build in 1903.

Shopping

BEADAZZLED
beadazzled.net
A playground for those who make their own jewelry, this store stocks a massive collection of beads, tools and books.
✚ E3 ✉ 1507 Connecticut Avenue NW ☎ 202/265-2323 🕐 Mon–Sat 10–8, Sun 11–6 Ⓓ Dupont Circle

BETSY FISHER
betsyfisher.com
Carrying designers like Nanette Lapore and Diane von Furstenberg, along with a few local designers, Betsy Fisher attracts women of all ages.
✚ F4 ✉ 1224 Connecticut Avenue NW ☎ 202/785-1975 🕐 Mon–Fri 10–7, Sat 10–6, Sun 1–5 Ⓓ Dupont Circle

BLUE MERCURY
bluemercury.com
Aside from its hard-to-match selection of hair- and skin-care products, Blue Mercury also sells Diptyque candles.
✚ E3 ✉ 1619 Connecticut Avenue NW ☎ 202/462-1300 🕐 Mon–Sat 10–8, Sun 11–6 Ⓓ Dupont Circle

CALVERT WOODLEY LIQUORS
calvertwoodley.com
In business for more than two decades, Calvert Woodley stocks DC's largest selection of wine as well as a range of fantastic cheese.
✚ D1 ✉ 4339 Connecticut Avenue NW ☎ 202/966-4400 🕐 Mon–Fri 10–8.30, Sat 9.30–8.30, Sun 10.30–5 Ⓓ Woodley Park–Zoo

CLAUDE TAYLOR PHOTOGRAPHY
travelphotography.net
Beautiful, evocative photographic prints from around the world.
✚ E3 ✉ 1627 Connecticut Avenue NW ☎ 202/518-4000 🕐 Mon–Sat 10–9, Sun 10–8 Ⓓ Dupont Circle

CROOKED BEAT RECORDS
crookedbeat.com
This Adams Morgan shop is the place to find new and used LPs covering all genres, from punk to reggae and soul.
✚ F2 ✉ 2116 18th Street NW ☎ 202/483-2328 🕐 Mon 1.30pm–8pm, Tue–Sat 12–9, Sun 12–7 Ⓓ Dupont Circle

GLEN'S GARDEN MARKET
glensgardenmarket.com
The deli here puts the emphasis on small, responsible brands, selling only regionally grown and made foodstuffs.
✚ E3 ✉ 2001 S Street NW ☎ 202/588-5698 🕐 Mon–Fri 10–10, Sat–Sun 9–9 Ⓓ Dupont Circle

GOOD WOOD
goodwooddc.com
This friendly U Street shop carries high-quality, reasonably priced furniture, homeware and vintage jewelry.
✚ G3 ✉ 1428 U Street NW ☎ 202/986-3640 🕐 Mon–Sat 12–7, Sun 12–5 Ⓓ U Street/African-American Civil War Memorial/Cardozo

HEMPHILL FINE ARTS
hemphillfinearts.com
This large gallery stocks an impressive array of American artists responding to socially relevant subjects.
✚ G4 ✉ 1515 14th Street NW, 3rd floor ☎ 202/234-5601 🕐 Thu–Sat 10–5 Ⓓ U Street/African-American Civil War Memorial/Cardozo

HOME RULE
homerule.com
The go-to store for kitchenwares, home decor and bath products that are distinct, useful and well-priced.
✚ G3 ✉ 1807 14th Street NW ☎ 202/797-5544 🕐 Mon–Sat 11–7, Sun 12–5.30 Ⓓ Dupont Circle, then 10-min walk

KRAMERBOOKS AND AFTERWORDS CAFÉ

kramers.com

This landmark bookstore/bar/brunch spot/late-night hangout is always buzzing with activity—from those browsing for their next read to those chatting over a casual meal.

E3 1517 Connecticut Avenue NW 202/387-1400 Daily 7.30am–1am, Fri–Sat 7.30am–3am Dupont Circle

MEEPS

meepsdc.com

Meeps sells well-priced vintage clothing from the 1950s onward.

F3 2104 18th Street NW 202/265-6546 Mon–Wed 12–7, Thu–Fri 12–8, Sat 11–8, Sun 11–6 U Street/African-American Civil War Memorial/Cardozo

MISS PIXIE'S

misspixies.com

Stocked with low-price antiques and vintage home furnishings, Miss Pixie's is a popular place to browse.

G2 1626 14th Street NW 202/232-8171 Daily 11–7 U Street/African-American Civil War Memorial/Cardozo

PROPER TOPPER

propertopper.com

Fashionable headwear is the main draw, but also come for myriad accessories and home decor.

F4 1350 Connecticut Avenue NW 202/842-3055 Mon–Fri 10–8, Sat 10–6, Sun 1–5 Dupont Circle

RIZIK'S

riziks.com

From evening wear through bridal wear to casual day clothes and coats and jackets, Rizik's has led the evolution of couture fashion in Washington.

F4 1100 Connecticut Avenue NW 202/223-4050 Mon–Sat 9–6 Farragut North

SECONDI

secondi.com

Washington's top stop for designer consignment. Brands include Chanel, Kate Space, Marc Jacobs, Prada and Louis Vuitton.

E3 1702 Connecticut Avenue NW, 2nd floor 202/667-1122 Mon–Tue 11–6, Wed–Fri 11–7, Sat 11–6, Sun 1–5 Dupont Circle

SECOND STORY BOOKS

secondstorybooks.com

If used books are your passion, start here. If you don't find your treasure, it may be in Second Story's warehouse.

E4 2000 P Street NW 202/659-8884 Daily 10–10 Dupont Circle

SMASH RECORDS

smashrecords.com

Vinyl, vintage clothes and a cool vibe. A knowledgeable staff are on hand to help you find your way around everything from hip-hop to hard core punk, disco to dub step.

F2 2314 18th Street NW, 2nd floor 202/387-6274 Mon–Thu 12–9, Fri–Sat 12–9.30, Sun 12–7 U Street/African-American Civil War Memorial/Cardozo

TABLETOP

tabletopdc.com

Sleek retro housewares are the calling card of this location. Items are well designed and priced as such, but be sure not to forget the bargain area in the back.

E3 1608 20th Street NW 202/387-7117 Mon–Sat 12–8, Sun 10–6 Dupont Circle

Entertainment and Nightlife

9:30 CLUB

930.com

See the most popular non-stadium acts take the stage at this well-designed club.

✛ H2 ✉ 815 V Street NW ☎ 202/265-0930 🕐 Hours vary, check online 🚇 U Street/African-American Civil War Memorial/Cardozo

BLACK JACK

blackjackdc.com

This upbeat bar offers pizza, inventive cocktails and a bocce court (a ball game similar to bowls or pétanque).

✛ G3 ✉ 1612 14th Street NW ☎ 202/319-1612 🕐 Tue–Thu 6pm–12am, Fri–Sat 5pm–1.30am, Sun 3pm–12.30am 🚇 Dupont Circle, then 10-min walk

BOHEMIAN CAVERNS

bohemiancaverns.com

The club has showcased performers such as Duke Ellington, and continues to attract jazz musicians.

✛ G3 ✉ 2001 11th Street NW ☎ 202/299-0800 🕐 Mon–Thu 7pm–midnight, Fri–Sat 7.30pm–2am, Sun 6pm–midnight 🚇 U Street/African-American Civil War Memorial/Cardozo

CAFÉ CITRON

cafecitrondc.com

Live Latin music and well-priced mojitos keep this spot popular.

✛ F4 ✉ 1343 Connecticut Avenue NW ☎ 202/530-8844 🕐 Mon 4–11, Tue–Thu 4pm–2am, Fri–Sat 4pm–3am 🚇 Dupont Circle

CHI-CHA LOUNGE

chichaloungedc.com

A plush lounge filled with sofas, Chi-Cha offers live Latin jazz, tapas, a tasty namesake drink and hookahs.

✛ F3 ✉ 1624 U Street NW ☎ 202/234-8400 🕐 Sun–Thu 5pm–11.30pm, Fri–Sat 5pm–1.30am 🚇 U Street/African-American Civil War Memorial/Cardozo, Dupont Circle

---

H STREET NE

This once gritty stretch of northeast DC has been reinvented as a nightlife scene that threatens to displace Adams Morgan and U Street. Go for tequila and mini golf at H Street County Club, German beers at Biergarten Haus, live music at Rock and Roll Hotel, signature cocktails at Atlas Room, DJs and dinner at Smith Commons, and beer and shots courtesy of The Pug.

EIGHTEENTH STREET LOUNGE

eighteenthstreetlounge.com

This multilevel house party is popular among Washington's most glamorous. You'll need to dress well.

✛ F4 ✉ 1212 18th Street NW ☎ 202/696-0210 🕐 Tue–Sun, check online for more details 🚇 Dupont Circle

SALOON

The Saloon prohibits standing and ordering martinis, but regulars find the beer list and the conversation inviting.

✛ E3 ✉ 1205 U Street NW ☎ 202/462-2640 🕐 Tue–Thu 11am–1am, Fri 11am–2am, Sat 2pm–2am 🚇 U Street/African-American Civil War Memorial/Cardozo

STUDIO THEATRE

studiotheatre.org

This independent company produces a season of classic and offbeat plays.

✛ G4 ✉ 1501 14th Street NW ☎ 202/332-3300 🚇 Dupont Circle

U STREET MUSIC HALL

ustreetmusichall.com

The 500-person limit here keeps things intimate, while one of the city's best sound systems keeps it loud.

✛ G3 ✉ 1115 U Street NW ☎ 202/588-1889 🕐 Hours vary, check online 🚇 U Street/African-American Civil War Memorial/Cardozo

Where to Eat

PRICES

Prices are approximate, based on a
3-course meal for one person.

$$$ over $50
$$ $30–$50
$ under $30

AMSTERDAM FALAFELSHOP ($)

falafelshop.com

Falafel and fries may be the only thing
on the menu here, but dozens of fresh
toppings make the difference.

⊞ F2 ✉ 2425 18th Street NW ☎ 202/234-
1969 🕐 Daily 11am–very late 🚇 Woodley
Park–Zoo, then 10-min walk

BEN'S CHILI BOWL ($)

benschilibowl.com

This U Street institution sells burgers,
hot dogs and fries to a late-night crowd.

⊞ G3 ✉ 1213 U Street NW ☎ 202/667-
0909 🕐 Mon–Sat breakfast, lunch, dinner, late
night; Sun lunch, dinner 🚇 U Street/African-
American Civil War Memorial/Cardozo

BRIXTON ($)

brixtondc.com

A British-style pub with regular happy
hours, the Brixton serves pub grub with
an interesting twist. The Lodge Bar has
brick-lined walls and a welcoming fireplace and the roof deck has great views.

⊞ H3 ✉ 901 U Street NW ☎ 202/560-5045
🕐 Mon–Fri 5pm–late, Sat 1pm–3am, Sun
12pm–late 🚇 U Street/African-American Civil
War Memorial/Cardozo

BUKOM CAFÉ ($)

bukomcafe.com

The spicy West African menu here is
filled with goat and lamb. There's live
African music nightly.

⊞ F2 ✉ 2442 18th Street NW ☎ 202/265-
4600 🕐 Daily dinner 🚇 Woodley Park–Zoo,
then 10-min walk

BUSBOYS AND POETS ($–$$)

busboysandpoets.com

This is the original location of DC's
favorite coffee shop, bookstore, restaurant, art gallery and performance space.

⊞ G3 ✉ 2021 14th Street NW ☎ 202/387-
7638 🕐 Sun 9am–midnight, Mon–Thu
8am–midnight, Fri 8am–1am, Sat 9am–1am
🚇 U Street/African-American Civil War
Memorial/Cardozo

CF FOLKS ($)

cffolksrestaurant.com

Art Carlson has presided over this
indispensable luncheonette since 1981.
Don't miss the daily specials.

⊞ E4 ✉ 1225 19th Street NW ☎ 202/293-
0162 🕐 Mon–Fri lunch 🚇 Dupont Circle

LE DIPLOMATE ($$$)

lediplomatedc.com

A reservation at this exceptional Parisian-
style brasserie has been coveted since
its critically acclaimed opening.

⊞ G3 ✉ 1601 14th Street NW ☎ 202/332-
3333 🕐 Daily dinner from 5pm, Sat–Sun
brunch 9.30–3, aprés-midi 3–5 🚇 Dupont
Circle, then 10-min walk

MULTICULTURAL

The city's multicultural makeup yields an enticing choice of ethnic restaurants. A walk along
18th Street leads past: **Bukom Café** (see this page); **Duken** (Ethiopian ✉ 1114–1118
U Street ☎ 202/667-8735); **Little Fountain Café** (International ✉ 2339 18th Street
☎ 202/462-8100); **Meskerem** (Ethiopian ✉ 2434 18th Street ☎ 202/462-4100); and
Mezè (▷ 94).

HANK'S OYSTER BAR ($$)

hanksoysterbar.com

This lively seafood stop serves up simple yet skillful dishes that draw your attention to the finest ingredients.

F3 ✉ 1624 Q Street NW ☎ 202/462-4265 ⏰ Daily lunch, dinner 🚇 Dupont Circle

INDIQUE ($$)

indique.com

Modern Indian food, a take on the American classics and creative cocktails make up Indique's menu.

Off map at D1 ✉ 3512 Connecticut Avenue NW ☎ 202/244-6600 ⏰ Mon–Thu dinner, Fri–Sun lunch, dinner 🚇 Cleveland Park

KOMI ($$$)

komirestaurant.com

Chef Johnny Monis draws people in with his basic, yet inspired, dishes crafted with exquisite ingredients. The cuisine has Greek influences.

F3 ✉ 1509 17th Street NW ☎ 202/332-9200 ⏰ Tue–Sat dinner 🚇 Dupont Circle

LEBANESE TAVERNA ($–$$)

lebanesetaverna.com

Specializing in Lebanese *meze*, this restaurant is known for its warm and welcoming hospitality.

E1 ✉ 2641 Connecticut Avenue NW ☎ 202/265-8681 ⏰ Daily lunch, dinner 🚇 Woodley Park–Zoo

MEZÈ ($–$$)

mezedc.com

This Turkish spot produces tasty *meze* as well as a full menu. There's a large selection of mojitos to choose from, which you can sample out on the roomy patio.

F2 ✉ 2437 18th Street NW ☎ 202/797-0017 ⏰ Daily dinner, Sat–Sun brunch 🚇 Woodley Park–Zoo

NORA ($$$)

noras.com

The nation's first restaurant to be certified as organic, Nora offers a menu of free-range meats and seafood in a dining room beautifully decorated with Amish quilts.

E3 ✉ 2132 Florida Avenue NW ☎ 202/462-5143 ⏰ Mon–Sat dinner 🚇 Dupont Circle

SATELLITE ($)

satellitedc.com

Fun California-style diner serving beer, burgers and alcoholic milk shakes.

H3 ✉ 2047 9th Street NW ☎ 202/506-2496 ⏰ Mon–Fri 5pm–close, Sat–Sun 11–4, 5pm–close 🚇 U Street/African-American Civil War Memorial/Cardozo

SUSHI TARO ($$–$$$)

sushitaro.com

This sushi powerhouse always has three grades of tuna on hand. Reserve a seat at the Omakase counter for an unparalleled dining experience.

F4 ✉ 1503 17th Street NW ☎ 202/462-8999 ⏰ Mon–Fri lunch, dinner, Sat dinner 🚇 Dupont Circle

TEAISM ($)

teaism.com

This simple teahouse offers an eclectic collection of Asian-inspired dishes and good-value Japanese bento boxes.

E3 ✉ 2009 R Street NW ☎ 202/667-3827 ⏰ Daily breakfast, lunch, dinner 🚇 Dupont Circle

THAI CHEF ($)

thaichefsushibardc.com

The kitchen here produces some of the best Thai food in town.

E3 ✉ 1712 Connecticut Avenue NW ☎ 202/234-5698 ⏰ Daily lunch, dinner 🚇 Dupont Circle

Exploring beyond the city center and its residential enclaves is well worth the subway or taxi ride. Historic sites, cultural institutions and acclaimed restaurants abound, as well as great shopping options.

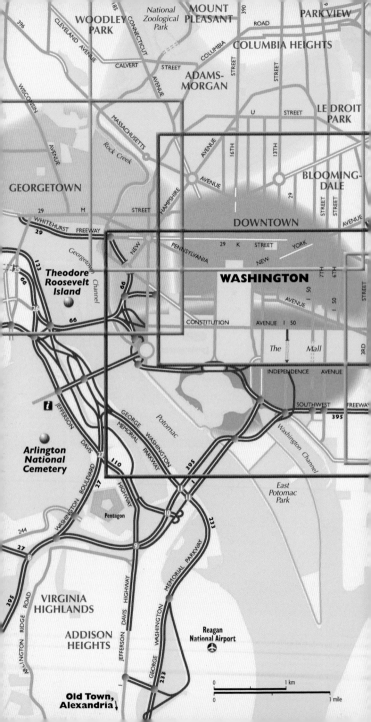

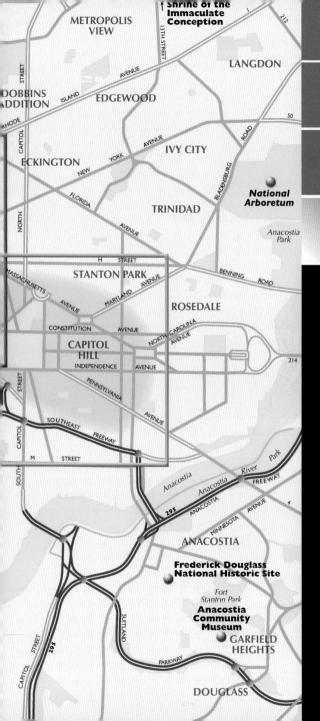

† **Shrine of the Immaculate Conception**

METROPOLIS VIEW

212

13TH STREET

LANGDON

AVENUE

DOBBINS ADDITION

ISLAND

EDGEWOOD

RHODE

CAPITOL STREET

50

ROAD

ECKINGTON

YORK

NEW

AVENUE

IVY CITY

BLADENSBURG

FLORIDA

NORTH

TRINIDAD

National Arboretum

Anacostia Park

AVENUE

H STREET

STANTON PARK

MASSACHUSETTS

MARYLAND AVENUE

BENNING ROAD

AVENUE

ROSEDALE

CONSTITUTION

AVENUE

NORTH CAROLINA AVENUE

CAPITOL HILL

214

INDEPENDENCE

AVENUE

STREET

PENNSYLVANIA

AVENUE

CAPITOL

SOUTHEAST

FREEWAY

SOUTH

M STREET

Anacostia River Park

Anacostia

FREEWAY

295

ANACOSTIA

MINNESOTA AVENUE

4

ANACOSTIA

Frederick Douglass National Historic Site

Fort Stanton Park

Anacostia Community Museum

GARFIELD HEIGHTS

295

SUITLAND

CAPITOL STREET

PARKWAY

DOUGLASS

Arlington National Cemetery

HIGHLIGHTS

- Kennedy graves
- Tomb of the Unknowns
- Custis-Lee Mansion
- L'Enfant's grave
- USS *Maine* Memorial
- Shuttle *Challenger* Memorial
- Astronauts Memorial
- Changing of the Guard at the Tomb of the Unknowns

TIP

- Remember that many visit to pay their respects. Dress appropriately and keep an eye on children.

The national cemetery since 1864, Arlington contains the most visited grave in the country, that of John F. Kennedy. Rows of white crosses commemorate the war dead and national heroes with dignity.

Lest we forget Veterans from every American war are interred here on the land of General Robert E. Lee's (1807–70) Arlington House. Those who fought and died before the Civil War were moved here after 1900. Perhaps the most famous soldiers to be buried here are those that have not yet been named. The Tomb of the Unknowns contains the remains of a World War I, World War II and Korean War soldier. A soldier from the Vietnam War was disinterred in 1998 after DNA evidence identified him. Sentries

Clockwise from left: The mast of Battleship Maine *surrounded by gravestones in Arlington National Cemetery; Changing of the Guard at the Tomb of the Unknowns; the rooftops of the city of Washington, viewed from the hillside of the cemetery; visitors among the graves and blossom-covered trees*

from the Third US Infantry guard the tomb 24 hours a day and perform the Changing of the Guard ceremony. Other memorials throughout the cemetery commemorate particular events or groups of people, including those killed in the Pentagon on September 11, 2001, and those aboard the Space Shuttle *Columbia* that crashed in 2003.

White markers and a flame Under an eternal flame, John F. Kennedy lies next to his wife, Jacqueline Bouvier Kennedy Onassis, and two of their children who died in infancy. Nearby lies his brother, Robert, whose grave is marked by a simple white cross and a fountain. The Custis-Lee Mansion sits above the Kennedy graves. Just off the house's west corner lies the grave of Pierre L'Enfant, the city's designer.

THE BASICS

arlingtoncemetery.mil

🕂 C8

✉ Across Memorial Bridge from Lincoln Memorial

☎ 877/907-8585

🕐 Apr–Sep daily 8–7; Oct–Mar 8–5

🎫 Free

♿ Excellent. Visitors with disabilities may board Arlington National Cemetery tour bus free of charge

🚇 Arlington Cemetery

❓ Tour bus service departs continuously from the Welcome Center. Changing of the Guard: Apr–Sep daily on the half hour; Oct–Mar daily on the hour

Frederick Douglass National Historic Site

TOP 25

The colonial-style exterior of Cedar Hill (left and opposite); inside Frederick Douglass's home (below)

Built in 1855, the Italianate country house known as Cedar Hill was the last home of abolitionist Frederick Douglass. Decorative arts, libraries and family mementoes provide an intimate look at his life and work.

Slave America's famous abolitionist was born into slavery in Maryland around 1818 and separated from his mother at birth. When Douglass was 12, his master's wife illegally taught him how to read. He escaped to Maryland when he was 20, becoming active in the Massachusetts anti-slavery movement. He wrote an autobiography in 1845, which became so popular that he had to flee to Europe out of fear that his former master would find out and he would be recaptured. There, British friends bought him his freedom, and he lectured widely on anti-slavery topics. When he moved into Cedar Hill, he was the first black resident of Anacostia, breaking the prohibition against "Irish, Negro, mulatto or persons of African blood."

Viewpoint Cedar Hill, now the Frederick Douglass National Historic Site, occupies the highest point in Anacostia, with a great view of the Anacostia River and the capital. At his rolltop desk in the library, Douglass wrote his autobiography *The Life and Times of Frederick Douglass*. The National Park Service, which manages the site, maintains a visitor center and a bookstore specializing in African-American titles.

More to See

ANACOSTIA COMMUNITY MUSEUM

anacostia.si.edu

This Smithsonian museum examines, documents and interprets the impact of historical and contemporary social issues on urban communities.

➕ See map ▷ 97 ⊠ 1901 Fort Place SE ☎ 202/633-4820 🕓 Daily 10–5 🚇 Anacostia, then bus W2, W3. Free weekend shuttle to Anacostia from the Mall Memorial Day to Labor Day 💷 Free

NATIONAL ARBORETUM

usna.usda.gov

The Arboretum's 446 acres (180ha) invite driving, biking and hiking. There's also the National Herb Garden, National Bonsai Collection and Azalea Walk.

➕ See map ▷ 97 ⊠ 3501 New York Avenue NE ☎ 202/245-2726 🕓 Fri–Mon 8–5. Weekend tram tours Apr–Oct 🚇 Stadium-Armory, then bus B2 💷 Free

OLD TOWN, ALEXANDRIA

A well-preserved colonial port town, Old Town's cobblestone streets are packed with early-American homes and taverns. Along the waterfront, tourists picnic as the boats come in.

➕ See map ▷ 96 ⊠ Old Town, Alexandria, VA 🚇 King Street–Old Town

SHRINE OF THE IMMACULATE CONCEPTION

nationalshrine.com

The largest church in the western hemisphere, this Catholic basilica is renowned for its mosaics and is dedicated to the Virgin Mary.

➕ See map ▷ 97 ⊠ 400 Michigan Avenue ☎ 202/526-8300 🕓 Apr–Oct daily 7–7; Nov–Mar 7–6. Tours Mon–Sat 9–3, Sun 1.30–3.30 💷 Free 🚇 Brookland CUA

THEODORE ROOSEVELT ISLAND

nps.gov/this

This island in the Potomac River has miles of walking trails through diverse terrain. A tall bronze statue of Roosevelt can be found in the center of the island.

➕ C5 ☎ 703/289-2500 🕓 Daily 6am–10pm 🚗 Car access from northbound lane of George Washington Memorial Parkway

Hydrangeas in the National Arboretum

The Theodore Roosevelt Monument on Theodore Roosevelt Island

Excursions

FREDERICKSBURG

The 40-block National Historic District in this charming Virginia town comprises the house George Washington (1732–99) bought for his mother, a 1752 plantation, the law offices of President James Monroe (1758–1831), an early apothecary shop owned by Hugh Mercer and the Georgian Chatham Manor, which overlooks the Rappahannock River.

Two Civil War battles were waged in and around town. You can now visit the battlefields and stroll through the nearby wilderness parks. Antiques and rare-book stores and art galleries line the streets. Start at the well-marked visitor center, which dispenses maps and advice.

THE BASICS

visitfred.com
Distance: 50 miles (80km)
Journey Time: 1–2 hours
🏢 706 Caroline Street
☎ 540/373-1776
🕐 Mon–Sat 9–5, Sun 11–5
🚆 Amtrak from Union Station
🚗 South on I-95 to exit 133A and follow signs to visitor center

GEORGE WASHINGTON'S MOUNT VERNON

This ancestral Virginia estate is the nation's second-most visited historic house after the White House. Washington worked this plantation's 8,000 acres (3,239ha) before he took control of the Continental Army and returned here for good after his presidency.

Washington supervised the expansion of the main house, most notably the addition of the back porch with a view over the Potomac. The mansion is built of yellow pine, painted multiple times with sand to resemble stone. The ornate interior is furnished with fine arts and memorabilia, and history interpreters provide more information. The outbuildings re-create the spaces of a self-sufficient, 18th-century farm, including the smokehouse and laundry, outside kitchen and slave quarters. Don't miss the view of George and Martha Washington's tomb, and allow time to explore the formal garden and follow the forest trail. The Ladies Association was founded in 1853 to preserve the estate.

THE BASICS

mountvernon.org
Distance: 15 miles (24km)
Journey Time: 40 minutes
☎ 703/780-2000
🕐 Apr–Oct daily 9–5; Nov–Mar daily 9–4
🚆 Huntington Station, then Fairfax Connector bus
🚗 Take 14th Street Bridge (toward National Airport), then south on George Washington Memorial Parkway
🚢 *Spirit of Mount Vernon* from Pier 4, 6th and Water streets SW (☎ 866/302-2469) Mar–Oct and Monday holidays
💰 Expensive

Shopping

FASHION CENTRE

Macy's and Nordstrom anchor the 170 stores in this Pentagon City mall.

🏠 Off map at C9 ✉ 1100 S Hayes Street at Army-Navy Drive and I-395 S ☎ 703/415-2400 🕐 Mon–Sat 10–9.30, Sun 11–6 🚇 Pentagon City

FRIENDSHIP HEIGHTS

These three shopping malls should fill any need. The upscale Mazza Gallerie and the Chevy Chase Pavilion across the street contain a range of shops including Neiman Marcus at Mazza. The über-chic Collection at Chevy Chase has Louis Vuitton and Cartier.

🏠 Off map at A1 ✉ Wisconsin Avenue at Western Avenue 🕐 Mazza Gallerie: Mon–Fri 10–8, Sat 10–7, Sun 12–6. Chevy Chase Pavilion: Mon–Sat 7am–11pm, Sun 7am–9pm. Collection at Chevy Chase: hours vary 🚇 Friendship Heights

HOUSE OF MUSICAL TRADITIONS

hmtrad.com

Musical instruments from lap dulcimers to bagpipes are sold at this well-known store, established in 1972.

🏠 Off map at J1 ✉ 7010 Westmoreland Avenue, Takoma Park, MD ☎ 301/270-9090 🕐 Tue–Sat 11–7, Sun–Mon 11–5 🚇 Takoma

POTOMAC MILLS MALL

One of Virginia's most popular destinations. Bargain shoppers will enjoy Banana Republic and Polo at a discount.

🏠 Off map at A9 ✉ 2700 Potomac Mills Circle, Woodbridge, VA ☎ 703/496-9330 🕐 Mon–Sat 10–9, Sun 11–6 🚌 Via I-95 S

TANGER OUTLETS

tangeroutlet/nationalharbor.com

Shop at over 85 brands then take in the other sites at the massive National Harbor development.

🏠 Off map at H9 ✉ 6800 Oxon Hill Road, National Harbor, MD ☎ 301/567-3880 🕐 Mon–Sat 9–9, Sun 10–7 🚌 5.5 miles (9km) via Interstate 295

TORPEDO FACTORY ART CENTER

torpedofactory.org

Pottery, paintings, jewelry, stained glass and other items by local artists, who work in the studios of this former US Naval torpedo station, are on display.

🏠 Off map at F9 ✉ 105 N Union Street, Alexandria, VA ☎ 703/838-4565 🕐 Daily 10–6, Thu til 9pm 🚇 King Street, then free trolley Sun–Wed 10am–10.15pm, Thu–Sat 10am–midnight

TYSONS CORNER

tysonscornercenter.com

Tysons Corner Center claims Nordstrom, Bloomingdale's and an AMC theater. Tysons Galleria, across the highway, is a little more upscale, with Saks Fifth Avenue and Chanel.

🏠 Off map at A2 ✉ 1961 Chain Bridge Road, Tysons Corner, VA ☎ 888/289-7667 or 703/847-7300 🕐 Center: Mon–Sat 10–9.30, Sun 11–7. Galleria: Mon–Sat 10–9, Sun 12–6 🚇 Tysons Corner 🚌 I-66 west to Route 7 west, then follow signs

ROYAL TREATMENT

Political staffers don't shirk from putting in their time at work, but they also know how to be pampered. Want to see partisans reeling from a recent loss or reveling in a clear victory? Head to: Aveda (☎ 202/965-1325), Blue Mercury (▷ 90), Grooming Lounge (▷ 29) or Roche Salon (☎ 202/775-0775). Many hotels, like the Mandarin Oriental (▷ 112), the Ritz-Carlton (▷ 112) and the Willard (▷ 112), have spas that give you the ultimate in superb treatments.

Entertainment and Nightlife

ARENA STAGE

arenastage.org

This company presents dynamically staged and superbly acted theater.

🔢 H8 ✉ 1101 6th Street SW ☎ 202/488-3300 🚇 Waterfront

BIRCHMERE

birchmere.com

One of America's top spots to catch the best bluegrass and folk acts.

🔢 Off map at D9 ✉ 3701 Mount Vernon Avenue, Alexandria, VA ☎ 703/549-7500 🕐 Check website for shows 🚇 Pentagon City, then taxi

CONTINENTAL

continentalpoollounge.com

This billiards hall is adorned with bright, retro decor and several cozy lounges, perfect for relaxing between games.

🔢 B5 ✉ 1911 North Fort Myer Drive, Arlington, VA ☎ 703/465-7675 🕐 Mon–Fri 11.30am–2am, Sat–Sun 6pm–2am 🚇 Rosslyn

THE FILLMORE

fillmoresilverspring.com

This opulent venue, with chandeliers and state-of-the-art sound system, dishes up regular well-known national acts. Be prepared to stand.

🔢 Off map at H1 ✉ 8656 Colesville Road,

Silver Spring, MD ☎ 301/960-9999 🕐 Box office Mon–Fri 12–6, Sat 11–4 🚇 Silver Spring

ROCK AND ROLL HOTEL

rockandrollhoteldc.com

A popular live-music venue that plays host to solid indie bands.

🔢 M5 ✉ 1353 H Street NE ☎ 202/388-7625 🕐 Daily 8pm–late 🕐 Check website for shows 🚇 Union Station, then 15-block walk

ROUND HOUSE THEATRE

roundhousetheatre.org

The Round House Theatre presents an eclectic set of professional plays.

🔢 Off map at A1 ✉ 4545 East-West Highway, Bethesda, MD ☎ 240/644-1100 🚇 Bethesda

SIGNATURE THEATRE

signature-theatre.org

This theater has become renowned for its sharply produced musicals, especially those of Steven Sondheim.

🔢 Off map at A9 ✉ 4200 Campbell Avenue, Arlington, VA ☎ 703/820-9771 🚇 Pentagon City, then taxi

STRATHMORE

strathmore.org

This major music venue has great acoustics. It hosts the Baltimore Symphony Orchestra and the National Philharmonic.

🔢 Off map at A1 ✉ 5301 Tuckerman Lane, North Bethesda, MD ☎ 301/581-5100 🚇 Grosvenor–Strathmore

WOLF TRAP

wolftrap.org

Wolf Trap draws top music acts, dance and musical theater to its outdoor amphitheater. When it's cold, shows take place in the Barns at Wolf Trap.

🔢 Off map at A1 ✉ Trap Road, Vienna, VA ☎ 703/255-1900 🚇 West Falls Church, then Wolf Trap express bus (in summer only)

Where to Eat

PRICES	
Prices are approximate, based on a 3-course meal for one person.	
$$$	over $50
$$	$30–$50
$	under $30

GRANVILLE MOORE'S ($$)
granvillemoores.com
Formerly a doctor's office, gastropub Granville Moore's now soothes with Belgian beers and mussels.
✚ M5 ✉ 1238 H Street NE ☎ 202/399-2546 ⏲ Mon–Fri dinner, Sat–Sun lunch, dinner 🚇 Union Station, then taxi or bus X2

GRAPESEED ($$)
grapeseedbistro.com
Choice is the word at this bistro/wine bar, where scrumptious dishes and delectable wines are available in small portions for tasting.
✚ Off map at A1 ✉ 4865 Cordell Avenue, Bethesda, MD ☎ 301/986-9592 ⏲ Tue–Fri lunch, Mon–Sat dinner 🚇 Bethesda

INN AT LITTLE WASHINGTON ($$$)
theinnatlittlewashington.com
An extravagant setting and an over-the-top American meal await the rich and famous who come here to sample chef Patrick O'Connell's kitchen and savor one of the 14,000 bottles of wine.
✚ Off map at A9 ✉ Main Street and Middle Street, Washington, VA ☎ 540/675-3800 ⏲ Daily dinner 🚗 I-66 and US-211 W

PHO 75 ($)
Pho, a Vietnamese noodle dish often eaten at breakfast in Vietnam, is served here in nearly 20 varieties—all of them tasty. Spoons are provided if you're not adept with chopsticks.

✚ A6 ✉ 1721 Wilson Boulevard, Arlington, VA ☎ 703/525-7355 ⏲ Daily 9–8 🚇 Rosslyn, then 10-min walk

RANGE ($$–$$$)
voltrange.com
Award-winning chef Bryan Voltaggio's restaurant draws food enthusiasts who come for the expertly cooked American fare. The bread basket has been called "one of the best in the city."
✚ Off map at B1 ✉ 5335 Wisconsin Avenue NW (Chevy Chase Pavilion) ☎ 202/803-8020 ⏲ Sun–Thu 11.30–10.30, Fri–Sat 11.30–11 🚇 Friendship Heights

RAY'S HELL BURGER ($)
rayshellburger.com
Connoisseurs highly rate the burgers served here. Reserve ahead or be prepared to wait.
✚ A6 ✉ 1650 Wilson Boulevard, Arlington, VA ☎ 703/841-0001 ⏲ Sun–Thu 11–10, Fri–Sat 11–11 🚇 Rosslyn, then 10-min walk

RAY'S THE STEAKS ($$)
raysthesteaks.com
This stripped-down and reasonably priced bistro focuses on serving some of the best steaks in town.
✚ A6 ✉ 2300 Wilson Boulevard, Arlington, VA ☎ 703/841-7297 ⏲ Daily dinner 🚇 Courthouse

RESTAURANT EVE ($$$)
restauranteve.com
The decor at Cathal Armstrong's restaurant, in an Eden theme, sets the stage for what comes next: Modern American cuisine that's truly inspired. Take your pick of courses from the tasting menus.
✚ Off map at F9 ✉ 110 South Pitt Street, Alexandria, VA ☎ 703/706-0450 ⏲ Bistro: Mon–Fri lunch, dinner, Sat dinner. Tasting menu, dinner only 🚇 King Street, then 20-min walk

With options ranging from the luxurious to simple budget hotels, Washington has a place to stay for everyone.

Where to Stay

Introduction

From those in town for all the free museums to deep-pocket lobbyists, from culture mavens to seekers of star chefs, Washington's hotels suit everyone.

Diplomats at Breakfast

The high-end and business-class hotels tend to be near the halls of power, whether at the White House or on Capitol Hill. Downtown and Georgetown play host to a fair share of luxury properties as well. There's a good chance that if you stay in one of the pricier digs you'll run into diplomats at breakfast and brush shoulders with heads of state (or their security guards) in the elevator or notice a Hollywood celebrity sitting in the bar, in town for a film shoot.

A Slower Pace

DC's smaller hotels and guesthouses are in the leafier areas of northwest DC. Guests in these areas will enjoy a slightly slower pace and smaller crowds, and the commute to the Mall and Hill is negligible.

Off Season? Not in DC

Summers bring tourists and winters bring policy makers and lobbyists. In fact, when Congress is in session, it's often more expensive to get a room during the week than on the weekend. Your best bet is to head for the suburbs, which are convenient for Metro stops.

WHERE THE PRESIDENTS LIVE

In the White House, correct? Not when it's being renovated. George Washington lived in New York and Philadelphia before the Capitol moved to DC. James Madison lived in the Octagon House (18th Street NW and New York Avenue) after the British burned the White House to the ground. Calvin Coolidge hosted Charles Lindbergh at the Patterson House (15 Dupont Circle) while the White House was being renovated. Harry S. Truman moved out for renovations also—to the nearby Blair House at 1651 Pennsylvania Avenue, where two Puerto Rican nationalists tried to assassinate him.

Budget Hotels

PRICES

Expect to pay up to $190 per night for a double room in a budget hotel.

ADAMS INN

adamsinn.com

This Victorian bed-and-breakfast encompasses three houses on a quiet street near Adams Morgan.

➕ F1 ✉ 1746 Lanier Place NW ☎ 202/745-3600 🚇 Woodley Park–Zoo, then 10-min walk

AMERICANA HOTEL

americanahotel.com

Step back in time at this family-owned hotel—the style is a throwback to the 1960s when it first opened.

➕ Off map at C9 ✉ 1400 Jefferson Davis Highway, Arlington, VA ☎ 703/979-3772 🚇 Pentagon City, Crystal City

EMBASSY ROW HOTEL

destinationhotels.com/embassy-row-hotel

You'll find this vibrant, stylish property in cosmopolitan Dupont Circle. It's well-known for its rooftop bar and pool.

➕ E3 ✉ 2015 Massachusetts Avenue NW ☎ 202/265-1600 🚇 Dupont Circle

GEORGETOWN INN

georgetowninn.com

Opened during the Kennedy presidency, this elegant hotel is at home amid the Federal-era architecture of its neighborhood. An outpost of the Daily Grille makes it a popular dining destination.

➕ C4 ✉ 1310 Wisconsin Avenue NW ☎ 866/971-6618 🚇 Foggy Bottom, then 15-min walk

HOTEL HARRINGTON

hotel-harrington.com

This is your basic, no-frills hotel in a great location. The Mall and many museums are just a few blocks away. There's also two restaurants and a pub.

➕ G6 ✉ 436 11th Street NW ☎ 202/628-8140 🚇 Metro Center

HOTEL TABARD INN

tabardinn.com

This charming old inn with plush rooms also sports a cozy lounge with a fireplace and a top-notch restaurant.

➕ F4 ✉ 1739 N Street NW ☎ 202/785-1277 🚇 Dupont Circle

KALORAMA GUEST HOUSE

kaloramaguesthouse.com

These Victorian town houses filled with 19th-century furnishings are near the Zoo and Adams Morgan.

➕ E2 ✉ 2700 Cathedral Avenue NW ☎ 202/588-8188 🚇 Woodley Park–Zoo

WINDSOR PARK HOTEL

windsorparkhotel.com

This charming hotel in a leafy suburb is just a short walk from Rock Creek Park. Free continental breakfast.

➕ E2 ✉ 2116 Kalorama Road NW ☎ 800/247-3064 🚇 Dupont Circle

WOODLEY PARK GUEST HOUSE

dcinns.com

This intimate bed-and-breakfast near the Zoo has individualized rooms filled with antiques. Young children are not allowed.

➕ D1 ✉ 2647 Woodley Road NW ☎ 866/667-0218 🚇 Woodley Park–Zoo

BED-AND-BREAKFAST

To find reasonably priced accommodations in small guesthouses and private homes, contact Bed & Breakfast Accommodations (✉ 1339 14th Street NW, Washington DC, 20005 ☎ 877/893-3233, bedandbreakfastdc.com).

Mid-Range Hotels

PRICES
Expect to pay between $190 and $325 per night for a double room in a mid-range hotel.

AKWAABA DC
akwaaba.com
A literary-themed luxurious bed-and-breakfast owned by the former editor of *Essence*, Akwaaba sits in a well-located town house.
F3 ✉ 1708 16th Street NW ☎ 202/328-3510 Ⓜ Dupont Circle

BEACON HOTEL
beaconhotelwdc.com
With a popular bar and grill, this lively hotel has well-sized, light-filled rooms.
F4 ✉ 1615 Rhode Island Avenue NW ☎ 202/296-2100 Ⓜ Dupont Circle

CAPITOL HILL HOTEL
capitolhillhotel-dc.com
Close to the Library of Congress and the Capitol, this family- and pet-friendly all-suites hotel encompasses two high-style buildings.
K7 ✉ 200 C Street SE ☎ 202/543-6000 Ⓜ Capitol South

EMBASSY CIRCLE GUEST HOUSE
dcinns.com/dupont-circle-bed-and-breakfast
Each room in this immaculately restored Georgian Revival mansion includes a private bath and a thick Persian rug.
E3 ✉ 2224 R Street NW ☎ 202/232-7744 Ⓜ Dupont Circle

THE FAIRFAX AT EMBASSY ROW
fairfaxhoteldc.com
On one of Washington's loveliest streets, the classically appointed Fairfax offers an elegant respite from the bustle of nearby Dupont Circle.
E3 ✉ 2100 Massachusetts Avenue NW ☎ 202/293-2100 Ⓜ Dupont Circle

THE GRAHAM GEORGETOWN
thegrahamgeorgetown.com
A conservative facade contrasts with the contemporary glamour found inside this property sited on a charming side street. The seasonal Observatory rooftop bar offers spectacular views.
D4 ✉ 1075 Thomas Jefferson Street NW ☎ 855/341-1292 Ⓜ Foggy Bottom, then 10-min walk

HENLEY PARK HOTEL
henleypark.com
A bit of Britain near the Washington Convention Center, this Tudor-style hotel serves formal tea each afternoon.
H5 ✉ 926 Massachusetts Avenue NW ☎ 202/638-5200 Ⓜ Mount Vernon Square, Metro Center

HOTEL MONACO
monaco-dc.com
Built in 1839 by the designer of the Washington Monument, Monaco has rooms with vaulted ceilings around a landscaped courtyard.
H5 ✉ 700 F Street NW ☎ 202/628-7177 Ⓜ Gallery Place–Chinatown

HOTEL PALOMAR
hotelpalomar-dc.com
This arts-themed Kimpton hotel hosts a wine-tasting every evening. The rooms are large and amenities plentiful, including a large outdoor pool.
E4 ✉ 2121 P Street NW ☎ 202/448-1800 Ⓜ Dupont Circle

HOTEL ROUGE
rougehotel.com
Decked out in rich reds and contrasting pale colors, Rouge appeals to style-savvy

visitors who value its location between the White House and Dupont Circle.
F4 ⊠ 1315 16th Street NW ☎ 202/232-8000 Ⓜ Dupont Circle

LIAISON CAPITOL HILL
affinia.com/liaison
The Liaison's prime location makes it ideal for visits to many of the major attractions. It has the largest rooftop pool and bar in the city.
J6 ⊠ 415 New Jersey Avenue NW ☎ 202/638-1616 Ⓜ Union Station

MARRIOTT WARDMAN PARK
marriott.com/WASDT
The huge, Victorian-style hotel rises above the Woodley Park Metro stop, which means there is a good view of Rock Creek Park. Amenities abound, as you would expect from a Marriott.
D1 ⊠ 2660 Woodley Road NW ☎ 202/328-2000 Ⓜ Woodley Park–Zoo

MORRISON-CLARK INN HOTEL
morrisonclark.com
Created by merging two 1864 town houses together, this gracious inn adds creative, modern touches to each guest room and public space. It is one of the Historic Hotels of America, recognizing its historic importance.
G4 ⊠ 1015 L Street NW ☎ 202/898-1200 Ⓜ Mount Vernon Square

THE NORMANDY HOTEL
thenormandydc.com
This European-style hotel, on a quiet embassy-lined street, is popular among diplomats. There's a wine and cheese reception in the evening and guests are given complimentary access to the fitness center and spa.
E2 ⊠ 2118 Wyoming Avenue NW ☎ 202/483-1350 Ⓜ Dupont Circle

THE PHOENIX PARK HOTEL
phoenixparkhotel.com
Bask in the aura and elegance of an 18th-century Irish estate steps away from the US Capitol. The Phoenix Park Hotel has served statesmen, tourists and diplomats since 1922.
J5 ⊠ 520 N Capitol Street NW ☎ 202/368-6900 Ⓜ Union Station

THE QUINCY
thequincy.com
These well-located suites offer quick access to the White House, Dupont Circle and Downtown.
F4 ⊠ 1823 L Street NW ☎ 202/223-4320 Ⓜ Farragut North

SWANN HOUSE
swannhouse.com
Converted from an 1883 Dupont Circle mansion, this bed-and-breakfast wows with feather beds, chandeliers and original molding.
F3 ⊠ 1808 New Hampshire Avenue NW ☎ 202/265-4414 Ⓜ Dupont Circle

TOPAZ HOTEL
topazhotel.com
Colorful Moroccan and Le Cirque influences complement the light, airy feel to this wellness-themed hotel, which provides in-room yoga equipment.
F4 ⊠ 1733 N Street NW ☎ 202/393-3000 Ⓜ Dupont Circle

WASHINGTON PLAZA
washingtonplazahotel.com
A resort like oasis located between Downtown and Logan Circle, this 1960s hotel was designed by Miami architect Mauris Lapidus. Guest rooms overlook the outdoor pool.
G4 ⊠ 10 Thomas Circle NW ☎ 202/842-1300 Ⓜ McPherson Square

Luxury Hotels

PRICES

Expect to pay more than $325 per night for a double room in a luxury hotel.

FOUR SEASONS HOTEL

fourseasons.com/washington

A gathering place for Washington's elite, this hotel features custom-made furniture and original artwork.

➕ D4 ✉ 2800 Pennsylvania Avenue NW
☎ 202/342-0444 🚇 Foggy Bottom

HAY-ADAMS HOTEL

hayadams.com

Looking like a mansion on the outside and an English country house within, this hotel has a picture-postcard White House view—ask for a room on the south side.

➕ F5 ✉ 800 16th Street NW ☎ 202/638-6600 🚇 McPherson Square

THE JEFFERSON

jeffersondc.com

Antiques and presidential paraphernalia can be found inside this Beaux Arts building, alongside modern amenities such as the huge glass bar in the center of the hotel's elegant lounge.

➕ F5 ✉ 1200 16th Street NW ☎ 202/448-2300 🚇 McPherson Square

MANDARIN ORIENTAL

mandarinoriental.com/washington

This large hotel, with a superb spa,

BOOKING AGENCY

Destination DC

A resource for finding hotels (both chain and boutique style), bed-and-breakfasts and campgrounds in the DC area. Either book online (washington.org) or call toll-free (800/422-8644).

---

features rooms with an Asian flare. The restaurants, Muze (▷ 52) and Empress Lounge, are popular.

➕ H7 ✉ 1330 Maryland Avenue SW
☎ 202/554-8588 🚇 Smithsonian

THE MAYFLOWER

themayflowerhotel.com

The lobby of this grand hotel glistens with gilded trim. The rooms have hosted many presidents, celebrities and royalty.

➕ F4 ✉ 1127 Connecticut Avenue NW
☎ 202/347-3000 🚇 Farragut North

RITZ-CARLTON, GEORGETOWN

ritzcarlton.com/georgetown

In spite of the fact this used to be an industrial building, this sleek hotel is luxurious and cozy.

➕ C4 ✉ 3100 South Street NW ☎ 202/912-4100 🚇 Foggy Bottom, then 15-min walk

ROSEWOOD WASHINGTON DC

rosewoodhotels.com

This hotel in Georgetown is right beside the C&O canal, and combines classic design with the latest technology.

➕ D4 ✉ 1050 31st Street NW ☎ 202/617-2400 🚇 Foggy Bottom, then 15-min walk

SOFITEL, LAFAYETTE SQUARE

sofitelwashingtondc.com

Sophisticated style and impeccable service are combined at this French-influenced hotel.

➕ G5 ✉ 806 15th Street NW ☎ 202/730-8800 🚇 McPherson Square

WILLARD INTERCONTINENTAL

washington.intercontinental.com

Heads of state have made the Willard Intercontinental their home since 1853. The Round Robin Bar is justly famous.

➕ G5 ✉ 1401 Pennsylvania Avenue NW
☎ 202/628-9100 🚇 Metro Center

This section takes you through all the practical aspects of your trip to make it run more smoothly.

Need to Know

Planning Ahead

When to Go

There is no bad time to visit Washington. Spring is busiest, when the city's cherry trees are in blossom. October and November bring brilliant foliage. Summer, although crowded and sweltering, sees a chockablock calendar of special events, many of which are free.

TIME

Washington is on Eastern Standard Time. Clocks go forward one hour in March and go back in late October.

AVERAGE DAILY MAXIMUM TEMPERATURES

	JAN	FEB	MAR	APR	MAY	JUN	JUL	AUG	SEP	OCT	NOV	DEC
	43°F	47°F	56°F	67°F	74°F	84°F	89°F	87°F	80°F	68°F	58°F	47°F
	6°C	8°C	13°C	19°C	23°C	29°C	31°C	30°C	26°C	20°C	14°C	8°C

Spring (mid-March to May) is extremely pleasant, with flowers and trees in bloom throughout the city.
Summer (June to early September) is hot and humid, with temperatures sometimes reaching 95°F (35°C) or more.
Fall (mid-September to November) is comfortable, and sometimes bracing.
Winter (December to mid-March) varies from year to year: It can be extremely cold or surprisingly warm. The occasional snowfall shuts the city down.

WHAT'S ON

January Antiques Show (washingtonwintershow.com).
Martin Luther King, Jr. Birthday Observations.
Restaurant Week (ramw.org/restaurantweek).
February Presidents' Day.
Chinese New Year's Parade (sometimes takes place in January).
March St. Patrick's Day Festival (shamrockfest.com).
Environmental Film Festival (www.dceff.org).
April National Cherry Blossom Festival

(nationalcherryblossomfestival.org).
White House Spring Garden Tour (whitehouse.gov).
Filmfest DC (filmfestdc.org).
May Passport DC (www.culturaltourismdc.org).
Memorial Day Concert.
June Capital Pride Festival (capitalpride.org).
Military Band Summer Concert Series (aoc.gov).
July Smithsonian Folklife Festival (festival.si.edu).
Independence Day (Jul 4, nps.gov).
Capital Fringe Festival (www.capitalfringe.org)

September National Symphony Orchestra Labor Day Concert (kennedy-center.org).
October Marine Corps Marathon (marinemarathon.com).
Taste of DC Festival (thetasteofdc.com).
November Veterans' Day.
December National Christmas Tree Lighting (thenationaltree.org).
You can find information about events in the area on the travel site washington.org.

Washington Online

si.edu
The Smithsonian Institution site features a directory of its 18 museums, schedules of events and exhibitons, information about publications and a link to the gift shop.

washington.org
This site is presented by the Washington DC Convention and Tourism board. You can make hotel reservations, gather information about the different neighborhoods and find out about annual events.

culturaltourismdc.org
The website of this nonprofit coalition of DC cultural and neighborhood organizations hosts comprehensive and easy-to-navigate listings of DC districts, walks, events and attractions that you might not be able to find elsewhere.

opentable.com
Allows diners to check availability and make reservations at most Washington restaurants.

washingtonpost.com
The newspaper's site features a going out guide, airport status reports, calendar of events and reviews of nightlife and restaurants.

washingtoncitypaper.com
The site of this alternative weekly carries the newspaper's superb arts and restaurant coverage, with reviews from the paper's critics and visitors to the site.

senate.gov and house.gov
Congress website including information on upcoming votes, history and how to visit.

goDCgo.com
This online hub of the District Department of Transportation (DDOT) provides everything you need to know about traveling by public transportation in DC.

TRAVEL SITES

fodors.com
A complete travel-planning site. You can research prices and weather; book air tickets, cars and rooms; ask questions (and get answers) from fellow travelers; and find links to other sites.

wmata.com
The Washington Metropolitan Area Transit Authority site features maps of the Metro and bus systems, plus information on delays and vacation schedules.

NEED TO KNOW PLANNING AHEAD

Getting There

AIRPORTS

DC is 1 hour 15 minutes from New York, 5 hours 40 minutes from Los Angeles and 6 hours 45 minutes from London. The major airports include Reagan National Airport, Dulles International Airport and Baltimore-Washington International Thurgood Marshall Airport (BWI).

FROM REAGAN NATIONAL AIRPORT

Reagan National Airport (tel 703/417-8000, mwaa.com) is in Virginia, 4 miles (6.4km) south of Downtown and the closest to central Washington. A taxi to Downtown takes about 20 minutes and costs around $15–$25. SuperShuttle (tel 800/258-3826, supershuttle. com) offers an airport-to-door service for $14 per person 24 hours a day. The blue and yellow Metro lines run from the airport to Downtown, with stations next to terminals B and C (Mon–Thu 5am–midnight, Fri 5am–3am, Sat 7am–3am, Sun 7am–midnight). Fare cards ($3.30) can be bought from machines on level 2 near the pedestrian bridges linking the two terminals. For Metro information call 202/637-7000.

RMA (tel 800/878-7743) will arrange for a car or limousine to meet you at the airport. The cost is around $150 for a sedan and $350 for a limousine, plus a 20 percent tip.

FROM DULLES INTERNATIONAL AIRPORT

Dulles International Airport (tel 703/572-2700, mwaa.com/dulles) is 26 miles (42km) west of Washington. A taxi to the city takes around 40

minutes and costs around $65. The Washington Flyer Coach (tel 888/927-4359) goes from the airport to the Wiehle–Reston East Metro. Buses leave the airport every 15–20 minutes Mon–Fri 6am–10.40pm, Sat–Sun 7.45am–10.45pm. The 10-minute trip costs $5 ($10 round-trip). SuperShuttle (tel 800/258-3826) costs $29 per person, plus $10 for each additional person. RMA (tel 800/878-7743) costs around $150 for a sedan and $350 for a limousine, plus a 20 percent gratuity.

FROM BWI AIRPORT

Baltimore-Washington International Thurgood Marshall Airport, its full title (tel 800/435-9294, bwiairport.com), is in Maryland, 30 miles (48km) northeast of Washington. A taxi from the airport takes around 45 minutes and costs $90. SuperShuttle (tel 800/258-3826) costs $37, plus $12 for each additional person. Free shuttle buses run between airline terminals and the train station.

Amtrak (tel 800/872-7245, amtrak.com) and MARC (tel 866/743-3682, mta.maryland. gov) trains run between the airport and Union Station. The 40-minute ride costs $15–$41 (depending on day and time) on Amtrak and $6 on MARC (weekdays only). With RMA you'll pay $150 for a sedan or $350 for a limousine, plus a 20 percent gratuity.

INSURANCE

Check your policy and buy any necessary supplements. It is vital that travel insurance covers medical expenses, in addition to accident, trip cancellation, baggage loss and theft. Also make sure the policy covers any continuing treatment for a more chronic condition.

ENTRY REQUIREMENTS

For the latest passport and visa information, look up the embassy website at uk.usembassy.gov. The authorities are now subjecting more people to even more security checks. To avoid problems allow plenty of time for clearing security, and be sure to check the latest advice. See also the panel opposite.

AIRLINES

Major air carriers serving the three airports (Reagan National Airport, Dulles International Airport and Baltimore-Washington International Airport) include:

Air Canada	☎ 888/247-2262	KLM Royal Dutch	☎ 866/434-0320
Air France	☎ 800/321-4538	Lufthansa	☎ 800/645-3880
British Airways	☎ 800/247-9297	Saudi Arabian Airlines	☎ 800/472-8342
Delta	☎ 404/773-0305	United	☎ 800/864-8331
El Al	☎ 800/223-6700	US Airways	☎ 866/428-4322
Frontier Airlines	☎ 800/432-1359	Virgin Atlantic	☎ 800/862-8621
Icelandair	☎ 800/223-5500		
Japan Airlines	☎ 800/525-3663		

For less expensive flights, contact:
Southwest Airlines ☎ 800/435-9792,
Spirit Airlines ☎ 801/401-2200 or
JetBlue Airways ☎ 800/538-2583.

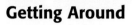

Getting Around

VISITORS WITH DISABILITIES

Museums and other public buildings are often equipped with ramps and elevators and are usually accessible to wheelchair users. Wheelchair access to Metro trains is via elevators from street level; details at wmata.com. Information on various DC locations can be found on individual websites.

CAPITAL BIKESHARE

The region's bike sharing service has more than 3,000 bicycles available at more than 350 stations in the area.
● Sign up online (capital bikeshare.com) and select from short- or long-term memberships ($10–$80).
● Take a bike from any Bikeshare station. Users must provide their own bike helmet.
● Return the bike to any Bikeshare station. Bikeshare is available year round.

PUBLIC TRANSPORTATION

● The subway (Metro) and bus (Metrobus) systems are run by the Washington Metropolitan Area Transit Authority (WMATA).
● Maps of the Metro system and some bus schedules are available in all Metro stations or at WMATA headquarters (600 5th Street NW).
● For general information call 202/637-7000, open Mon–Fri 6am–8.30pm, Sat–Sun 7am–8.30pm, wmata.com.
● The WMATA website is updated throughout the day showing problems on individual routes.
● For Lost and Found call 202/962-1195; for Transit Police call 202/962-2121.

BUSES

● Bus signs are blue, red and white.
● The bus system covers a much wider area than the Metro.
● The fare within the city is $1.75.
● Free bus-to-bus transfers are available when using a SmarTrip card and are good for about 2 hours at designated Metrobus transfer points.
● If you use cash, make sure you have the exact change as bus drivers don't carry money.
● A 7-day regional SmarTrip bus pass costs $17.50.

METRO

● The city's subway system, the Metro, is one of the cleanest and safest in the country. You need a farecard, called a SmarTrip card, loaded with money to pay the fare and to enter and exit the train area. Farecard machines, located in the stations, take coins and $1, $5, $10 and $20 notes. The most change the machine will give you is about $10, so don't use a large bill if you are buying a low-value card.
● Metro stations are marked by tall brown pillars with a large, white "M" at the top. A colored stripe under the "M" indicates the line or lines that are serviced by the station.
● Trains run every few minutes on Mon–Thu 5am–midnight, Fri 5am–3am, Sat 7am–3am, Sun 7am–midnight.

• The basic peak fare ($2.15) increases based on the length of your trip. It is cheaper at off-peak times. Maps in stations tell you both the rush-hour fare and regular fare to any destination station. A one-day pass is $14.50.
• Tap the SmarTrip card on the fare gate on entry and exit.

DC CIRCULATOR

• An alternative to the Metro, the large red buses of the DC Circulator run every 10 minutes on five routes connecting places of interest and cost only $1. Routes: Dupont Circle–Georgetown–Rosslyn; Georgetown–Union Station; Potomac Avenue Metro–Skyland; Union Station–Navy Yard; Woodley Park–Adams Morgan–McPherson Square. Full details of the routes and operating hours can be found on the website (dccirculator.com).

TAXIS

• Taxis are abundant and safe in Washington. Look for cars with white lights on their roof tops, which signal they are for hire. Fares are $3.25 upon entering the cab and 27 cents for each additional one eighth of a mile. Other charges that may be added include luggage at $0.50 a piece; if you're coming from the airport, there's an additional charge of $3; each additional passenger is $1.

DRIVING

• Driving in Washington is for the patient only.
• Although "right turn on red" is permitted, most Downtown intersections have signs forbidding it from 7am to 7pm, or banning it outright. Virginia also allows "left turn on red" when turning into a one-way street from another one-way street.
• The speed limit in the city varies from street to street; the maximum speed limit in residential areas is 25mph (40kph).
• Don't exceed the speed limits, as there are hidden cameras in popular areas.
• Seat belts are mandatory.

CAR RENTAL

Alamo ☎ 800/028-2390
Avis ☎ 800/633-3469
Budget ☎ 800/218-7992
Dollar ☎ 800/800-4000
Hertz ☎ 800/654-3131
National ☎ 877/222-9058
You will have to provide a credit card and drivers under 25 years old may have to pay a local surcharge.

PARKING IN DC

Parking is a problem in Washington, as the public parking areas fill up quickly with local workers' cars. If you park on city streets, check the signs to make sure it is permitted: Green and white signs show when parking is allowed, red and white signs when it is not. Parking on most main streets is not permitted during rush hours, and if you park illegally your car is likely to get towed. If it does, call ☎ 202/737-4404 to find out where it is and how to get it back. If it is towed on a weekend (after 7pm Friday) you'll have to wait until Monday to retrieve it.

Essential Facts

MONEY

The unit of currency is the dollar (= 100 cents). Notes (bills) come in denominations of $1, $5, $10, $20, $50 and $100; coins come in 25¢ (a quarter), 10¢ (a dime), 5¢ (a nickel) and 1¢ (a penny).

TAXES

Sales tax in Washington DC is 5.75 percent, hotel tax 14.5 percent (varies in Virginia) and food and beverage tax 10 percent.

BASIC NEEDS

Radio Shack sells voltage converters (732 7th Street NW and other locations, 202/638-5689; radioshack.com). For shoe repairs, try Cobbler's Bench (40 Massachusetts Ave NE and other locations; cobblers benchshoerepair.com).

CUSTOMS

● Visitors aged 21 or over may import duty free: 200 cigarettes or 100 cigars; 1 liter (1 US quart) of alcohol; and gifts up to $100 in value.
● Restricted import items include meat, seeds, plants and fruit.
● Some medication bought over the counter abroad may be prescription-only in the US and may be confiscated. Bring a doctor's certificate for essential medication.

ELECTRICITY

● The electricity supply is 110 volts AC, and plugs are standard two pins. Foreign visitors will need an adaptor and voltage converter for their own appliances.

EMBASSIES AND CONSULATES

● Canada at 501 Pennsylvania Avenue NW (tel 202/682-1740, can-am.gc.ca/washington).
● Ireland at 2234 Massachusetts Avenue NW (tel 202/462-3939, embassyofireland.org).
● UK at 3100 Massachusetts Avenue NW (tel 202/588-6500, gov.uk/government/world/organisations/british-embassy-washington).

EMERGENCY PHONE NUMBERS

● Police 911
● Fire 911
● Ambulance 911
● For all other non-urgent matters 311.

LOST PROPERTY

● Metro or Metrobus tel 202/962-1195
● Smithsonian museums tel 202/633-5630
● Other lost articles, call the city on 311.

MAIL

There are several post offices around the city:
● The North Capitol Station has the longest hours at 2 Massachusetts Avenue NE (tel 202/636-1259, open Mon–Fri 9–7, Sat–Sun 9–5).

- Farragut, 1800 M Street NW, tel 202/636-1259, Mon–Fri 9–5
- L'Enfant Plaza, 470 L'Enfant Plaza SW, tel 202/268-4970, Mon–Fri 8–5
- Washington Square, 1050 Connecticut Avenue NW, tel 202/636-1259, Mon–Fri 9–5
- Union Station, 50 Massachusetts Avenue NE, tel 202/636-1259, Mon–Fri 7.30–5, Sat 7.30–3.30.

MEDICAL TREATMENT

- The hospital closest to Downtown is George Washington University Hospital (900 23rd Street NW, tel 202/715-4000).
- Try Inn House Doctor for urgent care visits to Washington DC hotels (tel 202/216-9100 or ask at the front desk of your hotel).
- The DC Dental Society operates an online referral service (dcdental.org).
- Walgreens operates 24-hour pharmacies at 801 7th Street NW (tel 202/789-5345) and 1217 22nd Street NW (tel 202/776-9084).

MONEY MATTERS

- Credit cards are widely accepted in hotels, restaurants and shops, but some retailers may impose a surcharge.
- Tipping is expected for all services. As a guide the following applies:
Restaurants: 15–20 percent
Bartenders: 15 percent per round of drinks
Hairdressers: 15 percent
Taxis: 15 percent
Chambermaids: $1 per day
Porters: $1 per bag.

NEWSPAPERS AND MAGAZINES

- Washington has two major daily newspapers, *The Washington Post* and *The Washington Times*, which is more conservative.
- The *Washington City Paper*, a free weekly with an emphasis on entertainment, is available from newspaper boxes around town and at many restaurants, clubs and other outlets (washingtoncitypaper.com).

STREET NAMES

Washington's street names are based on a quadrant system, the center of which is the Capitol building. Numbered streets run north–south, while lettered streets run east–west. Both progress with distance from the Capitol. There is no "J" Street, eliminated to prevent confusion with "I" Street. For example, 1900 R Street NW is 19 blocks west and 17 blocks north of the Capitol, as "R" is the 17th letter if you skip "J." Diagonal avenues cut across the grid. They are named after the States based on their date of statehood and their proximity to the Capitol. Delaware, the "First State," is closest.

● In addition, various neighborhood weekly newspapers serve Capitol Hill, Georgetown, Adams Morgan and other areas.

● *Washingtonian*, a monthly magazine, has a calendar of events, dining information, arts reviews and articles about the city and its prominent people.

● *Where/Washington*, a monthly magazine listing popular things to do, is free at most hotels.

● Other national newspapers are available.

OPENING HOURS

● Stores generally open Mon–Sat 10–6, Sun 12–5.

● Banks open Mon–Fri 9–5, although hours can vary, with a handful open on weekends.

● Post offices open Mon–Fri 8–5, with some offices open Sat.

PUBLIC HOLIDAYS

● Jan 1: New Year's Day
● Third Mon in Jan: Birthday of Martin Luther King, Jr.
● Third Mon in Feb: Presidents' Day
● Last Mon in May: Memorial Day
● Jul 4: Independence Day
● First Mon in Sep: Labor Day
● Second Mon in Oct: Columbus Day
● Nov 11: Veterans Day
● Fourth Thu in Nov: Thanksgiving Day
● Dec 25: Christmas Day
● On public holidays banks and post offices close while many stores and restaurants stay open.

SMOKING

● DC is becoming less and less friendly to those who want to light up. Smoking is banned in almost all indoor public places, including restaurants, bars and clubs.

STATE REGULATIONS

● You must be 21 years old to drink alcohol in Washington, and you may be required to produce proof of age and photo ID.

STUDENTS
● Holders of an International Student Identity Card may be entitled to discounts at some clothing and electronic stores, theaters, cinemas and restaurants.

VISITOR INFORMATION
● Destination DC is at 901 7th Street NW, 4th Floor, Washington DC, 20001 (tel 202/789-7000, washington.org).
● Tourist Information is at 506 9th Street NW (tel 866/324-7386, downtowndc.org, Mon–Fri 8.30–5.30).
● National Park Service is at 1849 C Street NW, Washington DC, 20240 (tel 202/208-3818, nps.gov).
● National Park Service information kiosks can be found on the Mall, near the White House, next to the Vietnam Veterans Memorial and at several other locations throughout the city.
● The White House Visitor Center is located at Baldridge Hall in the Department of Commerce Building, 1450 Pennsylvania Avenue NW (tel 202/208-1631, nps.gov/whho, open daily 7.30–4).
● For recorded information on exhibits and special offerings at Smithsonian Institution museums, tel 202/633-1000.
● Discounted tickets for the theater, concerts, ballet, opera, cinema and galleries can be found at Ticketplace (ticketplace.org).

WASHINGTON SLANG
● "Hill staffers"—staff for individual members of Congress who work on Capitol Hill. Dominant demographic in DC.
● "Inside the Beltway"—the Beltway (I-495) forms a circle around the District. This refers to the American political system and its insularity.
● "Foggy Bottom," "Langley"—agencies are often referred to by their location. These are the State Department and CIA, respectively.
● "NoVa"—short for "Northern Virginia," this typically refers to Arlington and Alexandria. Occasionally used as a term of derision.

TELEPHONES
● To call Washington from the UK, dial 00 1, Washington's area code (202), and then the number.
● To call the UK from Washington, dial 011 44, then omit the first zero from the area code.

SAFETY
Washington is as safe as any large city, but the usual commonsense rules apply. Because of the wide income divide, crime statistics vary hugely from block to block. Tourist areas that are safe during the day may not be safe at night. At night walk with someone rather than alone; use taxis in less populous areas.

NEED TO KNOW ESSENTIAL FACTS

Timeline

EARLY DAYS

In 1779, President George Washington was authorized by Congress to build a Federal City. The following year, he hired Pierre Charles L'Enfant to design a city beside the Potomac River. According to legend, he sited the US Capitol in the exact middle of the 13 original states. By 1800, President Adams was able to occupy the unfinished White House, and Congress met in the Capitol, also unfinished. The population was by then around 3,000.

DOWN THE WIRE

In 1844, Samuel F. B. Morse transmitted the first telegraph message from the Capitol to Baltimore, Maryland.

1812 The US declares war on Britain in response to the impressment of sailors from American ships and border disputes in Canada.

1814 The British sack Washington, burning the White House and the Capitol. The war ends with the Treaty of Ghent, ratified in late 1814.

1846 Congress accepts James Smithson's bequest and establishes the Smithsonian Institution.

1850 The slave trade is abolished in the District of Columbia.

1863 President Abraham Lincoln's Emancipation Proclamation frees the nation's slaves; many move to Washington.

1865 Lincoln is assassinated during a performance at Ford's Theatre.

1867 Howard University is chartered by Congress to educate black people.

1876 The nation's centennial is celebrated with a fair in Philadelphia.

1901 The McMillan Commission oversees the city's beautification.

1907 Trains run to the new Union Station.

1922 The Lincoln Memorial is completed, 57 years after Lincoln's death.

1943 The Jefferson Memorial and Pentagon are completed.

1961 President John F. Kennedy plans the renovation of Pennsylvania Avenue. Residents are given the right to vote in presidential elections.

1974 The Watergate building becomes infamous as the site of the bungled Republican robbery attempt on Democrat headquarters. President Nixon resigns as a result of the ensuing cover-up.

1981 President Ronald Reagan is shot outside the Washington Hilton.

1991 Mayor Sharon Pratt becomes the first African-American woman to lead a major US city.

2001 Terrorists hijack a passenger plane from Dulles Airport on September 11 and crash it into the Pentagon, killing many people.

2009 Barack Obama, the first African-American president, is inaugurated.

2011 The Martin Luther King, Jr. Memorial is dedicated to the civil rights leader.

2015 District Councilwoman Muriel Bowser is sworn in as the seventh mayor of DC.

2016 The Smithsonian's groundbreaking National Museum of African American History and Culture (▷ 42–43) opens.

"I HAVE A DREAM"

On August 28, 1963, Martin Luther King, Jr. delivered his vision of racial harmony from the steps of the Lincoln Memorial to a crowd of 200,000. Born in 1929, King had entered the ministry in 1955. As pastor of the Dexter Avenue Baptist Church in Montgomery, Alabama, he became the figurehead of the organized non-violent civil-rights protests to end discrimination laws. His "I Have a Dream" speech ended a march on Washington by blacks and whites calling for reform. King was awarded the Nobel Peace Prize in 1964. His last sermon was at Washington National Cathedral in 1968—he was shot five days later in Memphis.

Below from left to right: Martin Luther King, Jr.; Smithsonian Institute; Union Station; Vietnam Memorial; George Washington

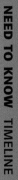

Index

Titles in the Series

- Amsterdam
- Bangkok
- Barcelona
- Boston
- Brussels and Bruges
- Budapest
- Chicago
- Dubai
- Dublin
- Edinburgh
- Florence
- Hong Kong
- Istanbul
- Krakow
- Las Vegas
- Lisbon
- London
- Madrid
- Melbourne
- Milan
- Montréal
- Munich
- New York City
- Orlando
- Paris
- Rome
- San Francisco
- Seattle
- Shanghai
- Singapore
- Sydney
- Tokyo
- Toronto
- Venice
- Vienna
- Washington, D.C.